PRAEGER LIBRARY OF U.S. GOVERNMENT DEPARTMENTS
AND AGENCIES

The United States Army

PRAEGER LIBRARY OF U.S. GOVERNMENT DEPARTMENTS
AND AGENCIES

Consulting Editors

ERNEST S. GRIFFITH

Former Dean and Professor Emeritus, School of International Service,
American University; former Director, Legislative Reference Service,
Library of Congress; and author of *The American System of Government* and *The American Government in Action*

HUGH LANGDON ELSBREE

Former Chairman, Department of Political Science, Dartmouth College; former Managing Editor, *American Political Science Review;*
former Director, Legislative Reference Service, Library of Congress

The United States Army

Vernon Pizer

LIEUTENANT COLONEL, USA (RET.)

FREDERICK A. PRAEGER, *Publishers*
New York · Washington · London

FREDERICK A. PRAEGER, *Publishers*
111 Fourth Avenue, New York, N.Y. 10003, U.S.A.
5, Cromwell Place, London S.W.7, England

Published in the United States of America in 1967
by Frederick A. Praeger, Inc., Publishers

Second printing, 1969

Why should men such as you, able to master the complex arts of science, mathematics, language, economy, and all the rest, devote their lives to a military career, with all of its risks and hardships? Why should their families be expected to make the personal and financial sacrifices that a military career inevitably brings with it?

When there is a visible enemy to fight in open combat, the answer is not so difficult. Many serve—all applaud—and the tide of patriotism runs high. But when there is a long, slow struggle, with no immediate visible foe, your choice will seem hard indeed . . .

But you have one satisfaction, however difficult those days may be: When you are asked, by a President of the United States or by any other American, what are you doing for your country, no man's answer will be clearer than your own.

JOHN F. KENNEDY

United States Military Academy
June 6, 1962

- How do the Reserves function?
- What sort of career and educational opportunities does the Army offer?

Colonel Pizer examines these and other questions from the point of view of the GI in the field, the official in the Pentagon, and the Commander in Chief in the White House. Discussing everything from how the foot soldier is supplied to the newest in "stability operations" in Viet-Nam and in computerized weaponry, he provides a clear and convincing picture of why today's Army is "the finest the nation has ever produced."

THE AUTHOR: Lieutenant Colonel Vernon Pizer, USA (Ret.), is the author of two earlier books, *Your Assignment Overseas* and *Rockets, Missiles, and Space*. He has also contributed to the *Saturday Evening Post, Reader's Digest,* and other national magazines.

A Note About the Seal on the Jacket Front:

The seal of the United States Army is the same used throughout the history of the United States by the War Office up to the time, in 1947, when the National Security Act eliminated the Department of War, creating the Department of the Army and the Department of the Air Force in the new Department of Defense. The then Secretary of War, Kenneth C. Royall, elected to retain for the Army the old seal first designated for the Board of War under the authorization of the Continental Congress on March 8, 1779, and Chief of Staff General Dwight D. Eisenhower approved the redesignation in September, 1947.

FREDERICK A. PRAEGER, *Publishers*
New York • Washington • London

THE UNITED STATES ARMY

Vernon Pizer
Lieutenant Colonel, USA (Ret.)

Praeger Library of U.S. Government
Departments and Agencies

Preface

The late President Kennedy posed the rhetorical question of why men serve in the United States Army. This book raises a series of collateral questions. How do men serve in the U.S. Army? What are the Army's missions, its roles, functions, and problems? How is the Army organized, trained, commanded, controlled, deployed, armed, equipped? What are its strategies and tactics? Why has the Army developed as it has? What influences and pressures have shaped its course? What is the tactical and strategic relationship of the Army to the other armed services? How does it handle its relationships with the Congress of the United States?

This is not a history of the U.S. Army, though much history is in its pages. Nor is it a technical treatise, although ground-force techniques are analyzed in detail. Nor is it a critique of military policy and its makers, although both come in for their share of attention. Rather, this book is intended to be an overall portrait of the Army as an agency of the U.S. Government.

Science is defined as a body of facts systematically arranged and interrelated in accordance with tested principles and doctrine. Because the profession of the man-at-arms conforms to that definition, it is accurately termed "military science." But a rigid and pedantic approach cannot do justice to a profession that is an art as well as a science, a profession in which the skills and talents of the practitioner, and the imagination and animation with which he practices, exert a penetrating influence. I have tried to cover my subject in a manner that is consistent with its twofold character, to treat the "body of facts systematically arranged" with imagination and animation.

In the course of working on this book, I enjoyed the wise counsel and assistance of many persons, and I am deeply grateful to each. Some, however, were so generous with their time and advice that a blanket expression of appreciation is insufficient recognition. Accordingly, I wish to acknowledge my debt to Colonel Edwin C. Gibson, Lieutenant Colonel Charles W. Burtyk, and Major B. J. Smith of the Office of the Secretary of Defense; Colonel Charles R. Cawthon of the National Guard Bureau; Joseph W. Penton of the Army Matériel Command; and Joseph A. Bourdow of the Office of the Chief of Information, U.S. Army. All of them are professional colleagues and good friends of long standing; for that reason, in addition to the demand imposed by accuracy, I wish to make it clear that none of them bears any responsibility for opinions expressed in the text or for such shortcomings as this book may reflect.

I suspect that authors' wives are often included in prefatory acknowledgments because this simple device affords writers an opportunity for enhancing domestic tranquillity with minimum effort. Disclaiming any such motive, I express my great gratitude to my wife, Marguerite, for her invaluable critical advice, her constant encouragement, and her sympathetic forbearance during the writing of this book.

—*Lieutenant Colonel* VERNON PIZER, *USA* (*Ret.*)

Washington, D.C.

Contents

Preface   vii

   I. TEN COMPANIES OF RIFLEMEN   3

  II. ROLES AND MISSIONS OF THE U.S. ARMY   16

 III. TODAY'S ARMY: THE VIEW FROM THE FIELD   30

 IV. TODAY'S ARMY: THE VIEW FROM THE E-RING   48

   V. THE QUICK AND THE DEADLY   72

 VI. LOGIC AND LOGISTICS   82

 VII. STRATEGY AND THE ARMY   91

VIII. STABILITY OPERATIONS   104

 IX. JOINT OPERATIONS AND THE COMBATANT
       COMMANDS   117

   X. THE GROUND-AIR CONFLICT   141

 XI. THE RESERVE FORCES   154

 XII. THE ARMY AND THE CONGRESS   164

XIII. THE ROAD AHEAD   171

Appendix I: THE REGULAR ARMY DIVISIONS   191

Appendix II: U.S. ARMY AREAS   192

Appendix III: ACTIVE ARMY INSTALLATIONS AND
MAJOR ACTIVITIES IN THE CON-
TINENTAL UNITED STATES (BY
ARMY AREA)   193

Bibliography   203

Index   207

LIST OF CHARTS

Chart 1 Infantry Division (ROAD)   43

Chart 2 Airborne Division (ROAD)   44

Chart 3 Armored Division (ROAD)   45

Chart 4 Mechanized Division (ROAD)   46

Chart 5 Airmobile Division (ROAD)   47

Chart 6 Organization of the Department of the Army 60

Chart 7 Organization of the Office,
            Chief of Legislative Liaison (OCLL)   169

A section of photographs follows page 118.

The United States Army

I

Ten Companies of Riflemen

On June 14, 1775, the Second Continental Congress, meeting in the colony of Pennsylvania, voted to raise ten companies of riflemen to become the regular force of the Continental Army. Although it would not assume the name until 1789, the United States Army had been created with that gesture. Destined to defend a country not yet born and a people singularly unenthusiastic about regular armies—their own or anyone else's—the Army came into being in a way that left an imprint evident to this day.

The Congress reflected the prides, the prejudices, and the separate heritages of the colonial peoples it served. Never very far from the thoughts of the delegates was an inherited distrust of standing armies resulting from the misfortunes that many colonists or their forebears had suffered at the hands of the military in the lands of their origin. And the delegates were troubled by divided allegiances—loyalty to the specific colony they represented, loyalty to the nebulous concept of a union of the colonies, loyalty to the English Crown. Most of them had not yet abandoned hope that a way might still be found to restore effective and peaceful relations between the colonies and England.

But the Congress had convened only three weeks after the armed clashes between colonial militia and British troops at Lexington and Concord, only two weeks after the Provincial Congress of Massachusetts had voted to raise a local force of 13,600 men and had called on the other colonies for aid in resisting the British. On the very day the delegates gathered, Ethan Allen and eighty-three of his Green Mountain Boys struck across Lake Champlain to capture the British-manned Fort Ticonderoga. The past could not be undone, nor could its direction be reversed. The Continental Congress was carried along on an impetus not its own, in a direction it was not at all certain it wanted to take. On May 15, it adopted a resolution placing the colonies in a state of defense. Two weeks later, John Adams proposed to his fellow delegates that the colonial militia besieging the British headquarters in Boston be accepted as the Continental Army. In another two weeks, on the same day that it established a regular military force, the Congress designated a five-man committee to draft regulations for the administration of the Continental Army, thereby establishing at the outset a pattern of civilian control of the military that has never been abandoned or even seriously challenged. The following day, by unanimous vote, the legislators named George Washington to the post of Commander in Chief. Before another week had passed, Congress had appointed three major generals to serve under Washington and had adopted its first military appropriations bill, providing the sum of $2 million in bills of credit for the support of the Army.

How depressed Washington must have been on the morning of July 3, when, at Cambridge Common, outside Boston, he assumed command of "all continental forces, raised or to be raised, for the defense of American liberty." That stirring phrase of the Congress was devoid of any real meaning. The ten Regular rifle companies existed solely on paper; recruiting for them was just beginning. The only Regulars physically present in the Continental Army were the Commander in Chief and his three major generals. To be sure, the militia was in being, but in Washington's own words, it was "a broken staff." The militiamen were poorly trained, poorly equipped, poorly led, and dedicated to the idea of marching back to their farms and forges as soon as their six-month enlistments expired.

Ultimately, Washington's forces mauled the British and their mercenaries and secured a new nation in the New World. But eight grueling years separated the victory in 1783 from that July morning. During those trying years—years of battles won and battles lost, of blunder and brilliance, of hardship and frustration and courage—the Continental Army was molded into a fighting force even as it waged war.

Washington's problems when he assumed command would have crushed a lesser person. His men were undisciplined, ornery, rambunctious, disdainful of conformity, convention, and constraint. They fought as individuals rather than as a unit. For the most part officers were commissioned by the colonial governors as a reward for political services rendered. With discouragingly few exceptions, they lacked experience or aptitude for tactical planning or for command of combat troops. No adequate supply system existed—and, had there been one, it seems probable that niggardly political leaders would have provided few supplies for the system to service. Above all, the Continental Army had no cohesive identity, little *esprit de corps,* and small will to endure until final victory, come hell or Hessians. The men did not know, any more than the rest of the country, what they were really fighting for. Would victory mean a return to a liberalized form of colonial government, or the establishment of a form of government in which America was coequal with England under the supreme power of the Crown, or the establishment of a new and independent form of government in which the effective power resided in the people? The grand objective of the war did not emerge clearly until July 4, 1776. Then the Declaration of Independence helped give the country and the Continental Army purpose and direction. But most of all, it was Washington himself who gave the Army a sense of identity and a determination to win. Largely by the force of his personality and his deep grasp of the character of his men, he was able slowly to infuse his soldiers with spirit. Even as he badgered Congress for greater material support, he worked to inspire his men to make the most effective use of what they had.

The situation was not completely disheartening. General Washington's soldiers were not without assets. While carving out homes in a wilderness, they had learned to cope with the Indians and the elements—both largely inhospitable. They came to fight knowing the advantages of cover and concealment, a stealthy approach, dispersal instead of bunching into a lucrative target. The difficulty of securing fresh stocks of ammunition in remote areas had taught them to make their shots count, to aim instead of firing in mass volleys that were often more sound than fury. From the start, there was well-founded hope that these soldiers could become an army if they could be disciplined, if they could be taught to maneuver and to think as units instead of as individuals, if competent leaders could be developed, and if Congress and the public would provide adequate material support.

The first significant help for Washington in his herculean task came from abroad. Most European countries were between wars. Scores of professional officers, restless under their unaccustomed inactivity, sought commissions in the American army. Some were self-seekers, some adventurers, some genuinely moved by the struggle of a colonial people with the temerity to try to cast off the yoke of monarchy. Regardless of motive, all found their way to the Continental Congress, where they beseeched the delegates for suitable roles in the war. To clear its doorstep of these foreign volunteers, Congress commissioned most of them. Washington's staff swelled with senior officers for whom he often could not find suitable employment. But out of this multilingual pool came the Marquis de Lafayette, Louis Duportail, Thaddeus Kosciuszko and Count Casimir Pulaski, Baron Johann de Kalb and Baron Friedrich Wilhelm von Steuben. In Lafayette, Washington had a competent commander, a brave and inspiring officer, and a powerful influence with the French court, which later sent an expeditionary force under Count Jean Baptiste de Rochambeau in response to Lafayette's pleas. Duportail and Kosciuszko, experienced engineers, constructed excellent defensive fortifications. Pulaski was a top cavalry commander; he later fell mortally wounded in an attack on the British at Savannah. De Kalb was a tough, dedicated infantry commander; he was killed leading his troops at Camden. And, in von Steuben, Washington had an indefatigable, brilliant work horse of an officer who left an indelible mark on the U.S. Army.

Von Steuben, more than anyone else, instilled the necessary discipline. He drew up the first manual of arms and, until he could develop training officers to assist him, personally formed up the troops and led them out to the field, where he drilled them tirelessly until their response to a crisp command was flawless and automatic. He established a standardized, maneuverable battalion of 200 men in place of units of assorted sizes. He pressed for a single basic infantry weapon. He created in the American soldier a willingness and a capability to use the bayonet, a weapon previously ignored. (In passing, it might be noted that, to this day, soldiers regard with something less than enthusiasm two of von Steuben's innovations: nightly bed checks and Saturday morning inspections.) It was during his unrelenting drilling of the troops that von Steuben discovered an attribute of American soldiers that set them apart from European men-at-arms—the American insisted on knowing why. Von Steuben considered that "the genius of this nation" is that "I am obliged to say, 'That is the reason why you ought to do that,' and then he [the American soldier] does it."

Washington also had home-grown officers of distinction. General Henry Knox, a Boston bookseller before the war, commanded American artillery with verve and great ability. "Light Horse Harry" Lee was a daring, skillful cavalry commander. Washington himself organized the light infantry, a highly mobile force of marksmen who struck fast and hard; among his best light infantry commanders were Alexander Hamilton and Alexander Scammel, both courageous and highly proficient. Commanding larger units in the field were many effective senior officers, including Anthony Wayne, Daniel Morgan, and—until his inglorious defection—Benedict Arnold. In Nathanael Greene, Washington found a quartermaster general who knew how to organize a logistical system and who had the fortitude to browbeat reluctant merchants and farmers into exchanging needed goods and produce for Continental promissory notes (giving rise to the scoffing expression, "not worth a Continental").

Over them all for eight long years of war was Washington, the leader who composed differences among his officers and restored harmony among his often unpaid and often unfed troops, the military commander who planned over-all strategy, the diplomat who cajoled the Continental Congress and local leaders into making men and money available and who, ultimately, persuaded the Congress to authorize three-year enlistments—although one year continued to be par for actual service. Washington became, in essence, the conscience and the soul of the Continental Army and of the fledgling nation itself.

In 1783, the war was over. And now, paradoxically, an army that had wrested victory from the enemy faced defeat at the hands of the nation it had fought to establish. Displaying characteristic uneasiness about maintaining a standing military establishment in time of peace, on November 2, 1783, the Continental Congress ordered the Continental Army to disband.

Groping for a Formula

Although the Congressional delegates adopted an edict to abolish the Army, their sentiments were not as fixed and definitive as their action. In this, they reflected a curiously American ambivalence concerning the military—an attitude that has not yet disappeared. One body of opinion, supported by General Washington and those closest to military affairs, was convinced that the security of the nation could be guaranteed only by the continued existence of an adequate, trained army, immediately available to meet threats from any quarter. A second body of public opinion, dazzled by exaggerated legends of the invincibility of the armed and aroused citizen-soldier, placed reliance upon a "people's army," a loose arrangement of part-time militia to be mobilized only in event of imminent danger.

Deeply concerned for the safety of his country and searching for a formula to reconcile the two opposing views, Washington proposed a compromise in his "Sentiments on a Peace Establishment." Modifying his wartime disenchantment with an "armed citizenry," he endorsed a people's militia and the principle of a nation in arms. But at the same time, he proposed that the first line of defense be a regular army. Recognizing that a large peacetime establishment was an unattainable goal in the context of the times, he suggested a modest strength of 2,631 officers and men organized in four regiments of infantry and one of artillery. In his "Sentiments," Washington also advanced a basic principle that was later to be used around the world to support universal conscription and total war: "It may be laid down as a primary position and the basis of our system, that every citizen who enjoys the protection of a free Government, owes not only a proportion of his property, but even of his personal services to the defense of it."

The professional counsel of the former Commander in Chief notwithstanding, Congress reiterated its order for dissolution of the Continental Army, expressing the view that "standing Armies in time of Peace are inconsistent with the principles of republican government." At the same time, contradicting itself in at least a technical sense, Congress authorized retention of eighty soldiers on active duty to guard military stores. For one year this feeble, token force constituted the entire army. Then in 1785, the delegates authorized the enlistment of 700 men to be organized in one regiment of infantry and two companies of artillery. (The regiment exists today as the 3d Infantry, the senior regiment in the U.S. Army.)

Four years later, when Washington took the oath of office as the first President, army strength stood at 672. If the same ratio of soldiers to total population were maintained today, the

U.S. Army would number less than 35,000, or approximately one-thirtieth the number of civilians employed by the present military establishment. In 1790, the authorized strength was raised to 1,283.

The ups and downs of its early years established an enduring pattern for the U.S. Army. In times of emergency the Congress (representing the will of the people) responded to threats from abroad by granting the Army, in haste and often in confusion, the support it should have been permitted to absorb in effective, orderly fashion in time of peace. And when the emergency ended, Congress and the nation, still reluctant to maintain a large standing military force in peacetime, cut back support sharply, although the Army still had to discharge responsibilities.

Certainly, the post-Revolution U.S. Army did not lack responsibilities. Chief among them was the duty of preserving law and order on the frontier and protecting settlers migrating westward. To accomplish this, patrols probed deeper and deeper inland from the eastern seaboard, building a string of posts in strategic areas, exploring the broad expanse of the continent, and fighting countless engagements against hostile tribes bent on stemming the accelerating encroachment of the settlers.

Although the Army had its hands full trying to pacify the Indians, it embarked on an experimental reorganization in 1792, in which it converted itself into a "legion" divided into four "sublegions," each composed of eight companies of infantry, four companies of rifles, one troop of dragoons (cavalry), and one battery of artillery. The experiment was abandoned in 1796 in favor of conventional regiments and battalions, and a short time later the brigade and division concept was added. But while it lasted, the legion made its contribution, largely because of the character of its commander, General Anthony Wayne. "Mad Anthony," crotchety and ill-tempered though he might have been, was a taskmaster in the von Steuben tradition. He drilled and trained and toughened his troops ceaselessly until, in the end, he had created a disciplined, effective force. It was this force, skillfully employed by Wayne, that defeated the Indians at the Battle of Fallen Timbers, thereby ensuring the security of the northwestern frontier.

In 1802, still groping for a formula that would satisfy a young democracy's reluctance to maintain a peacetime military establishment, Congress ordered a limitation of two infantry regiments and one artillery regiment. In the same year, it authorized the founding of the United States Military Academy at West Point, in accord with a proposal originally put forth by Henry Knox in 1776 and later urged by Washington, Alexander Hamilton, and Thomas Jefferson. But the legislators yielded to the pleas for the academy more in form than in substance. Administration of the institution was placed under the newly formed Corps of Engineers. The faculty was limited to five and the student body to ten. No provision was made for suitable facilities.

The War of 1812

In 1812, the United States embarked on a war against England that never should have been. It was a futile war that gained nothing, neither glory nor practical profit, for either side. At the outbreak of hostilities, the U.S. Army numbered less than 7,000 Regulars. It was woefully short of competent commanders—a consequence of the vacillation, the confusion, and the often contradictory orders with which the politicians had hamstrung the Army since the end of the Revolution. Fortunately, the U.S. Navy was in a condition to take to the sea with some assurance. However, it was not at sea but on land that the outcome of the fighting was to be determined.

Faced with a war for which it was ill-prepared, the Army could hope only to minimize the harsh consequences; it could not hope for stunning victories. Having involved the country in war (by a margin of only six votes in the Senate), Congress now demonstrated its military ineptitude by requiring the Army to place major reliance upon the hodgepodge of the state militias, despite the lessons of the Revolution. The war was not lost, as well it might have been; nor was it won, as under the circumstances it could not have been. It ended in 1814 in a negotiated peace.

West Point Emerges from the Doldrums

The one positive result of the inglorious War of 1812 was belated recognition of the need for supporting the Army and, in turn, a change in Congressional indifference to West Point. Congress authorized a more adequate faculty for the academy, fixed the strength of the Corps of Cadets at 250, and prescribed admission standards. But then, as though exhausted by the effort to put West Point on a firm footing, the legislators in 1815 failed to appropriate operating funds, and the superintendent was forced to borrow funds privately to keep the academy solvent until Congressional fingers could be pried loose from their purse strings.

In 1817, Major Sylvanus Thayer assumed the superintendency of West Point. Breathing vitality into the institution, he broadened and strengthened the curriculum to suit the needs of a professional army, upgraded the faculty and the teaching techniques, nurtured the critical and analytical talents of the students, and, above all, insisted on adherence to standards of integrity that were uncompromisingly high. One of Thayer's most fortunate acts was the appointment of Dennis Hart Mahan to the faculty. Mahan taught for forty-one years and made a profound contribution to military science. Under his influence, three major concepts were embraced: detailed study of past campaigns and tactics, recognition of the necessity for command flexibility in adapting lessons of the past to the realities of the present, and adoption of the doctrine of the offensive as the likeliest path to victory. Mahan's operational principles emphasized thorough reconnaissance, sound tactical disposition, and rapid and skillful maneuver.

The effect of West Point upon the military establishment, and upon the country as a whole, was tremendous. With increasing numbers of cadets graduating into the officer corps, a new level of professionalism emerged. More than merely a military institution, the academy was the nation's leading school of science and engineering until midway in the nineteenth century; in fact, for much of the period it was the only organization worthy of such a designation. Consequently, the nation called on West Pointers for many services not contemplated when the academy had been founded. For more than a quarter of a century, beginning in 1827, with the Baltimore and Ohio, Army units commanded by West Pointers were assigned significant roles in the construction of every major railroad in the country. They surveyed routes for canals and aqueducts, constructed public works of every description, initiated a river-and-harbor improvement program, and even directed the erection of the north and south wings of the Capitol.

To some degree, the Army became a victim of the academy's success. The nation was now on the eve of the industrial revolution, and private interests importuned West Pointers to resign their commissions in order to develop and supervise the emerging industrial technology. It was a situation not unlike that caused by the industrial-scientific revolution 100 years later, wherein private enterprise sought to attract military specialists into expanding aerospace, electronics, and nuclear programs. In the nineteenth century, as in the twentieth, a number of officers laid their uniforms away in mothballs, but by far the greater number remained in military service. In either case, the nation was the beneficiary.

The Army Matures

In 1846, the effectiveness of the U.S. Army on the field of battle was put to the test with the outbreak of the Mexican War. On the eve of hostilities, authorized strength stood at 8,600, but actual strength was less than 7,000. Congress, repenting in haste for past neglect, voted increases that more than doubled the number of Regulars and empowered the President to accept a maximum of 50,000 volunteers. This time, having finally learned that militiamen controlled by and responsive to individual states were frequently more liability than asset, the 50,000 volunteers were to be enlisted into *national* service. But, having plugged one hole, the legislators opened another by authorizing one-year terms of enlistment, thus sharply curtailing the usefulness of the volunteers. Mexico, at the outbreak of war, had approximately 32,000 Regulars under arms, a territorial militia, and the advantages of familiarity with terrain and climate.

The U.S. Army fought the war under a number of handicaps. More than once, on the verge of mounting an important operation, commanders would suffer the bitter vexation of watching the bulk of the volunteer force dribble away and head home, their short-term enlistments having expired. Often, needed supplies would be immobilized in the North for lack of transportation. Sometimes, commanders in the field were forced to twiddle their thumbs in helpless frustration as they waited for their indecisive masters in Washington to approve their battle plans. But, for all that, the U.S. Army in Mexico was distinguished by much that approached, and sometimes achieved, sheer military brilliance—imaginative use of artillery, daring maneuver, skillful reconnaissance, the first employment of a large-scale amphibious operation, and the highly competent leadership of a score of officers, among them Generals Winfield Scott, Zachary Taylor, and John E. Wool, and —on a less exalted level—Captains Robert E. Lee, J. E. Johnston, and George B. McClellan. One significant development of the war was the demonstration that citizen-volunteers, if they could be kept free of the divisive and enervating influence of the state militia and if they could be gotten into battle before their enlistments expired, responded to decent training and leadership by fighting well.

In September, 1847, the Mexicans surrendered. The U.S. Army had fought and won its first major foreign war. There would be more wars in the future—the tragedy of the Civil War, the *opéra bouffe* Spanish-American War, the holocausts of the two world wars, the bitter Korean War, and the equally bitter war in Viet-Nam. But this much was already certain: the U.S. Army had come of age. It had developed leadership, professionalism, character, and impetus. Despite the various vicissitudes and frustrations it might face in the years ahead, the Army was now firmly established as a trained, responsible, resourceful force. It had survived Congressional and public attitudes that sometimes went beyond indifference and suspicion to border on outright hostility. It had surmounted the inequity of being deprived of the men and matériel needed to match its responsibilities. George Washington had once said, "Let us have a respectable army, and such as will be competent to every exigency." The Army that emerged in the 1850's would have found favor in the eyes of its first Commander in Chief.

II

Roles and Missions of the U.S. Army

To a generation that has come of age in a world ruptured by a nonstop series of wars, it may seem superfluous to raise the matter of the Army's mission. Against a martial background, the subject would appear to require no explanation. And in the abstract, divorced from the specifics of a given situation, it requires none. The classic mission of the U.S. Army is far from obscure: to provide the land power necessary to preserve the security and to support the national purpose of the United States. Having said that, to say no more is to take refuge in a convenient catch phrase that has the virtue of brevity and the fault of inadequacy. However, to appreciate the implications of the mission and to understand the many roles of the Army, it is necessary to look behind the catch phrase.

Title 10, Section 3062, of the United States Code reads in part:

> It is the intent of Congress to provide an Army that is capable
> . . . with the other Armed Forces, of preserving the peace and
> security . . . of the United States; . . . supporting the national
> policies; implementing the national objectives; . . . and over-
> coming any nations responsible for aggressive acts that imperil
> the peace and security of the United States.

The United States Code makes it quite clear that there is a duality to the official mission of the Army. The first segment is clearly part and parcel of the soldier's job—the preservation of peace and security by repelling and defeating aggression. But the second portion is not so clear and unequivocal. Aggression is definable and recognizable—a shot fired, a bor-

16

der breached, a harbor blockaded, a hostile missile poised in a neighboring country. But national policies and national objectives—in other words, the nation's purpose—are another story. A nation's purpose is difficult to pin down with precision. Even pinned down, it assumes first one shape and then another. And the Army is expected to reflect these changes.

In other words, the Army must reflect the public will. It must do whatever the country in its collective wisdom wishes. There can be no quarrel with that principle—only support for it. But often when there has been no thunder of guns in the air, the nation has appeared to forget the Army's obligations of "preserving the peace and security" and "overcoming any nations responsible for aggressive acts." The Army's needs in assuming and maintaining a state of combat readiness have been neglected, and the obligations of "supporting the national policies" and "implementing the national objectives" taken as a mandate to heap high the chores that have sometimes dissipated the Army's ability to fight promptly and effectively.

At times, the nation seemingly has been capricious or illogical in the assignment of tasks to the Army. Sometimes relying on naïve trust that danger from abroad would always remain remote, sometimes overpowered by the temptation to get "productive" work from such an "unprofitable" enterprise as a military force, sometimes yielding simply to the availability of a body of men accustomed to taking orders, the country has burdened the Army with a variety of supplemental missions bearing little or no relationship to the military purpose of an armed force. Thus, at different periods, obedient to its obligation of "supporting the national policies," the U.S. Army has found itself cast in strange and sometimes contradictory roles. In the early 1800's, it was frequently employed as an agency for the capture and return of runaway slaves; in 1865, it was ordered to establish and operate the Freedmen's Bureau to feed, clothe, house, educate, and advise former slaves. The Army has been utilized to apply leverage in labor disputes. It has been used in land reclamation, youth programs, public health projects, and many other undertakings in support of national policy. But were these assignments compatible with the Army's obligation to maintain itself as a fighting force, or did they not, to an extent, vitiate the Army's military posture? Although whatever has a beneficial effect on the country as a whole also has a beneficial effect upon the Army, it is not necessarily good for the Army to be the instrument for securing beneficial results. For example, judicial authorities have sometimes advocated that salvageable criminals guilty of lesser offenses should be taken into the Army for rehabilitation. But is it wise for a military force devoting its time and energies to the accomplishment of military objectives to be asked to wrestle with society's ordinary peacetime problems?

Even in the purely military realm, the nation has demonstrated ambivalence in sometimes wanting a big army, sometimes a little one, sometimes a citizen army, at other times a professional force. The young United States wanted its army to be an instrument for pacification of the Indians and for expansion westward. In later years, the nation used its army as a rod to rap the knuckles of the recalcitrant "banana republics," as a juggernaut to crush war machines run wild abroad, as governor and guardian of defeated peoples. The U.S. Army has been asked to be a gendarme walking an international beat, a mere appendage in the era of massive nuclear retaliation, a military missionary fighting bitter "nonwars" in distant places. Each role, each change of emphasis, has demanded of the Army a responsive modification of its character, its structure, its capabilities, its tactics, and its concepts. Often the changing roles have not been accompanied by the provision of adequate means to discharge additional duties without weakening the Army's capability for the accomplishment of its basic mission. And often, in response to the changeable nature of the national purpose, the overriding reason for maintaining an army has been all but obscured by the quasi-military—or even unmilitary—objectives with which its central mission has been overlaid.

To a greater extent than its sister services, the Army has been kneaded and thumped by the masseurs of the national purpose. The Navy, smaller and less diverse than the Army and with the advantage of the ocean as its natural medium, has not been subjected to as much conceptual change. The Air Force, short on history but long on glamour and bolstered by an effective lobby, has been subjected to relatively little tampering. The envy with which the Army has often regarded the other services is easily understood.

In time of war, the nation has never experienced difficulty in discerning the fundamental reason for having an army and in demanding of that army fulfillment of a responsibility for which suitable preparation in peacetime has not always been permitted. Only recently has the public recognized the need to permit its military plant to make in peacetime the investment required to keep it modernized—even though the "business" will show no "profit." An indication of changed attitudes was the placing of Job Corps camps in 1965 under civilian administration, whereas in 1933 the Army was assigned the task of operating more than 1,300 Civilian Conservation Corps camps. At last, the nation seems to have learned to check its impulse to cram new and unrelated roles and missions into the soldier's knapsack.

Combat Capability

To the Army's credit, it should be pointed out that peripheral tasks have seldom blinded it to its essential purpose. The obligation to provide the ground force required for support of the national will translates, in military terms, into a combat capability to seize and hold terrain coveted by the enemy. No matter how it is amplified or embroidered, an army's operational mission in war boils down to denying to the enemy that portion of the world's landscape that is in contention. To accomplish this purpose, the U.S. Army holds to the principle that the soldier is the key to victory, that the man with his feet on the ground and a gun in his hands is the ultimate arbiter in conflict. The Army believes that man is the decisive weapon.

The Navy and the Air Force employ complex mobile weapons systems—ships and planes—that engage the enemy in an environment where the protagonists are transient. Neither attacker nor defender is a creature of the sea or air; he is a visitor from the ground, and to the ground he returns. When weapons systems that contend successfully in a transient medium are turned against land targets, their effects may be dissipated with the smoke of their attack. Only soldiers (or U.S. Marines fighting as soldiers) are still there after the smoke lifts. The Navy won great sea battles in the Pacific in World War II, but soldiers and Marines had to seize and hold the ground, bloody island by bloody island, to force a final decision. The Air Force won great air battles and struck heavy blows against ground targets in Europe during World War II and later in Korea, but it was the man on the ground who finally settled the issue.

However, although land power is the decisive factor in war, unless supported by sea power and air power it can be defeated by the enemy. An army has the ability to force war to its ultimate conclusion, but without adequate naval and air support, that conclusion can be long delayed and can be less satisfactory than desired when finally attained.

In brief, the role of the U.S. Army in war is to supply the land power necessary to defeat the enemy; the Navy's is to supply the sea power; the Air Force's to supply the air power. In the sense that victory over an enemy depends upon seizing and holding ground, the mission of U.S. forces as a whole is geared to the Army's function, and the Army's fundamental mission may be said to hold unique significance for national survival.

The Army Between Wars

By its inherent nature, an army is an instrument for wreaking destruction in an organized and methodical manner, and the usual measure of its accomplishment is the speed and thoroughness with which it can destroy an enemy. But this is not the whole story; it is only the most obvious chapter. Paradoxically, nearly all armies have their constructive side. From its inception, the U.S. Army has played a remarkably positive role between wars in contributing to the welfare of the nation, over and above its function of ensuring security from hostile forces. Some of the contributions have been a civilian "spin-off" from the Army's constant probe for methods of enhancing its capabilities for purely military pursuits. Some are the consequence of assigning the Army tasks it alone could perform well because of the unique capabilities it had acquired essentially for military purposes. In both cases, the contributions of the Army to the national well-being have been positive and plentiful.

Chronologically, exploration was the Army's initial peacetime contribution to implementing national objectives—and the Army both stimulated and promoted expansion of the nation. In 1803, the United States negotiated the Louisiana Purchase, possibly the most stupendous real estate transaction in history. For $15 million, the country received title to some 1 million square miles stretching from the Mississippi River and the Gulf of Mexico westward to "beyond the mountains." Both buyer and seller were fairly evenly matched in their ignorance of the physical characteristics of that vast territory more than one-quarter the size of the entire European continent. It was the U.S. Army's task to find out what the country had bought. More specifically, it was the task of Captain Meriwether Lewis, Lieutenant William Clark, four sergeants, twenty-three privates, and several guides and Indian interpreters.

Setting out in May, 1804, the expedition moved westward from the Missouri River through land no white man had previously penetrated, reaching the Pacific Ocean eighteen arduous months later. On the return trip, the party split itself into two teams so that it could cover twice as much ground. When the two teams regrouped at the Missouri two and a half years after they had commenced their odyssey, the explorers had covered 8,000 miles, acquiring for the nation its first authentic knowledge of the geography, the climate, the resources, and the tribes of the region, and drawing the first maps. Even before Lewis and Clark had returned, First Lieutenant Zebulon Pike had set out with a party of twenty soldiers to explore the headwaters of the Mississippi. For nine months they charted the river and then, in 1806, they turned their attention to the Red and Arkansas rivers. These daring expeditions, and other Army exploration that followed, opened up the West to settlement. Later, when the country acquired Alaska, it was the story of the Louisiana Purchase all over again. Once more it was the Army that performed the lion's share of the exploration—surveying routes, devising means of coping with the hostile elements, charting the trackless expanse, gathering data on climate, people, animals, and vegetation.

The Army has never laid away the mantle of the explorer. As recently as 1962, an Army team was dispatched to Antarctica on a mapping expedition. This time the party could use sophisticated scientific and technical aids undreamed of when Lewis and Clark were toiling over the Rockies. But not even those aids were as sophisticated as the devices the Army has had to invent for a current project—laboratory exploration of the moon. The detailed, large-scale maps the Army is preparing of a planet almost a quarter of a million miles distant embrace difficulties of consummate complexity; yet, nobody—least of all officials of the National Aeronautics and Space Administration, who are counting heavily on the maps for moon-landings—doubts the Army's ability to come through.

The Army has done more than simply explore the face of the nation; it has also created many of the features that give that face its distinctive appearance. In addition to assisting in the layout and construction of every railroad established during the first fifty years of national life, it was the Army that built the Capitol, the Washington Monument, Fort Dearborn (better known today as Chicago), the Panama Canal, bridges and roads beyond counting, installations supplying one-fifth of the country's total hydroelectric power, telegraph and cable systems, and the Alaska Highway. The Army is still building the nation, being charged by Congress with responsibility for a civil works program that includes, among other things, improvement of ports and inland waterways, flood control, and construction of major federal structures. Under this program the Army, through its Corps of Engineers, has constructed and maintains 300 coastal harbors and nearly 30,000 miles of waterways—the world's most extensive navigable system.

Not only is the Army's indelible imprint on the face of the nation, but its mark is everywhere within the industrial complex that is the cornerstone of the national strength and wealth. The Army, in fact, was largely responsible for creating, in the musket manufacturing facilities it established in Springfield, Massachusetts, in 1794, the mass production system that is the hallmark of industrial America. During the first year of production, the Army turned out 455 muskets—no insignificant feat in those days for the initial output of a modest plant. But it envisioned a much larger operation that could produce thousands rather than hundreds. With this in mind, in 1798 it contracted with Eli Whitney, the inventor of the cotton gin, for 10,000 muskets to supplement Springfield's production. The quantity was so large that it required initiation of new techniques to make it manageable. The system devised was a combination of the division of labor—to break the manufacturing process into repetitive, specialized segments—and the institution of unprecedented standards of uniformity and precision to provide identical, interchangeable parts. It established the pattern for assembly lines of the future.

Some time later, the Army helped industry in another way by establishing the first national meteorological system and the first daily weather reports. Throughout the network of Army posts, personnel were utilized as part-time observers, and their reports were flashed cross country via the Army's communications web. In 1891, the Army system became the Weather Bureau of the Department of Agriculture.

At a steadily accelerating pace, particularly during the twentieth century, the Army's influence has been felt in virtually every industry in the nation—from agriculture to metallurgy. In many cases, all that private plants have had to do has been to adopt for commercial production and civilian consumption the fruits of Army development programs. In other cases, industry has devised new products and innovative techniques largely in response to prodding by the Army. The public as a whole has been the beneficiary of developments as diverse as they are numerous. A random sampling turns up such varied items as antifouling paints (to prevent accumulation of barnacles on ship hulls), synthetic rubber, shrinkage prevention techniques for textiles, a pesticide to eliminate the boll weevil, the ubiquitous "jeep," all-climate lubricants, an improved helicopter rotor blade, a special coating to improve the effectiveness of optical lenses, and fire-resistant clothing.

As a matter of fact, entire industries owe their existence, at least in part, to the stimulation and support of the Army. Aviation commenced as a commercial undertaking when the Army placed an order for its initial airplane in 1908. Follow-on orders, eventually measured in terms of thousands of craft, plus the Army's insistence on increasingly rigid standards of reliability and performance, forced the industry to mature rapidly.

The communications-electronics industry is perhaps equally indebted to the Army for much of its growth and sophistication. For example, the basic patent for radar was issued to an Army officer. Especially significant have been the Army's pioneering efforts in the field of miniaturization of radio equipment, which led directly to the development of printed circuitry and transistors, and in turn, resulted in the advent of exotic computers. No less exotic is the instrumentation of space satellites; the Army led the way in devising the out-of-this-world techniques, just as it led the nation into the age of space with the successful launching of the first American earth satellite, Explorer I, in 1958.

The Army has also played a prominent part in the development of another of the modern world's most sophisticated fields—nuclear energy. Military prominence in this area dates back to early World II when the Manhattan Project, under which the first atomic bomb was produced, was supervised by an Army general. After the war, the Army undertook a continuing program to discover constructive uses for the awesome atom. From this program have come such beneficial results as lightweight, portable nuclear power plants that produce electricity in remote areas that would otherwise be without that all-important form of energy. Even more exciting is a revolutionary use developed by the Army for what has been one of the most feared aspects of the atom: radioactivity.

Some fifteen years ago, Army scientists embarked on a project to turn radioactivity into an ally of man. They sought to do this by shaping radioactivity into a means of feeding man better. Food spoils because of the growth within it of the spoilage-inducing bacteria that are always present. Traditional methods of food preservation—canning, freezing, drying, pickling, smoking—retard the growth of bacteria but they change the nature and the taste of the food. It has been altered from its fresh state into a product that has been precooked or that is dependent upon a freezer to remain edible. The Army's pioneer program has proven that controlled irradiation of foodstuffs can sterilize them by inhibiting the growth of bacteria without altering the natural, fresh state of the food and without in any way endangering the consumer. The proof of the pudding is in the eating, and for several years soldiers, as well as scientists and researchers, have been eating selected irradiated foods on a test basis—for instance, radiation-preserved loins of pork that have been kept on the shelf at room temperature for two years prior to cooking. (The uniform reaction of the diners has been to go back for seconds.)

The immediate military objective in undertaking this radical program has been to improve the soldier's year-round diet regardless of his location and to lessen the logistical load by a dramatic reduction of spoilage en route to the soldier. The potential benefits for the public are tremendous. The U.S. Food and Drug Administration, monitoring the program, has already approved several irradiated food items for unrestricted public consumption.

Always preoccupied with the search for improving the soldier's situation, the Army has naturally been closely concerned with the field of medicine, and providing the soldier with the highest possible standards of health care has greatly influenced the well-being of the public at large. There is seemingly no end to the Army's contributions to medicine, starting in 1800 when an Army surgeon led the way in overcoming smallpox in the United States by introducing mass vaccination to the military. Two years later, another Army doctor wrote the first American textbook on psychiatry. But it was in 1822 that the Army received its first world-wide acclaim for medical accomplishment. In that year, Army surgeon William Beaumont saved the life of a frontiersman accidentally shot in the stomach. The wound did not close—and through the opening Dr. Beaumont was able to make detailed studies of the processes of digestion. His precise, unique reports on the nature of digestion led Sir William Osler, an internationally famed medical authority, to hail him as the "pioneer physiologist of the United States and the first to make a contribution of enduring value."

Scores of Army contributions of enduring value followed: discovery of the organism that causes pneumonia, a means of preventing beri-beri, a vaccination to suppress typhoid epidemics, more effective means of treating shock and burns, better prosthetic appliances, basic findings on malaria, hookworm, amoebic dysentery, and dengue fever. Best known and most widely hailed of all U.S. Army medical accomplishments is the conquest of yellow fever. In 1900, four Army doctors, among them Major Walter Reed, were assigned the mission of investigating the disease that had been a scourge for centuries. Their studies convinced them that yellow fever could be transmitted only by the bite of a specific mosquito. In carefully controlled experiments in which soldier-volunteers permitted

themselves to become infected, the quartet of doctors successfully proved the validity of their theory. Two of the soldiers
sacrificed their lives in the experiments, but their deaths led to
the saving of untold millions.

Another important peacetime role of the U.S. Army is in
combating the effects of natural disasters. Because of its widespread deployment and mobility, the Army is able to respond
rapidly to a call of distress from any quarter; because it is
highly trained, organized, and well equipped, it is also able to
respond beneficially. Thus, in the tragic San Francisco earthquake and fire of 1906, less than one hour after the disaster
struck, the first troops were on hand battling flames and rescuing trapped victims. Hard on their heels came Army demolition experts to blow up buildings where necessary to stem the
onrushing flames. Army signalmen set up emergency communications systems, engineers dug into the muck and debris to
repair ruptured water mains, medical personnel established
emergency aid stations, quartermasters put up refugee tent
cities and field kitchens, and soldiers patrolled to guard against
looting. So prompt and effective were these military measures
that the civil authorities asked the Army to remain in charge
of all relief operations until the situation had resumed a
measure of normalcy. There is no way to calculate the number
of lives saved and the amount of suffering and property loss
prevented.

To the drama of San Francisco can be added Army disaster
relief operations in such widely separated points as Galveston,
Texas, in the great flood of 1915; Puerto Rico in the vicious
hurricane of 1926; the Mississippi and Ohio River valleys in
the floods that struck in 1912 and again in 1937; Texas City
in the waterfront explosion that claimed 500 lives in 1947;
and Alaska in the tragic earthquake and tidal wave that struck
in 1964.

The Army operations in the Alaskan emergency illustrate
its versatility in coping with the several concurrent crises that
accompany a natural disaster. The violent quake hit at 5:36

P.M. on March 27, 1964. Although military installations in Alaska were themselves disrupted by the fury of nature run wild, by 6:00 P.M. the first soldiers were on the scene in Anchorage and elsewhere to render vitally needed assistance to the stricken state. Army teams fanned out to dig through the rubble to free trapped victims. For several hours, the sole link between Anchorage and the outside world was a military police radio car parked near the city's public safety center; meanwhile, Army signalmen worked alongside civilian repair crews to restore the crippled communications networks. Military doctors and nurses set up emergency aid stations and worked twelve-hour shifts to minister to the injured. Army water trailers and water purification units were rushed into place, and soldiers began immediate stop-gap repairs to water and sewage lines. Generators, food, clothing, medicines, blankets, and other necessary supplies were brought in from military stocks. Army helicopters criss-crossed the damage area rescuing marooned families.

At the request of the civil authorities in Alaska, the Army's Corps of Engineers made a thorough assessment of the damages in the state, and rushed to completion comprehensive plans for restoration of public utilities systems, removal of debris and dismantling of unsafe structures, and repair of community facilities. As soon as these immediate projects were under way, the Army teams devoted themselves to other urgent reconstruction problems, among them the restoration of the harbor complexes and the rebuilding of twenty damaged schools. One tricky problem facing the Army was to determine where new construction should be located in order to minimize vulnerability to any future quakes; to do this, the Corps of Engineers sank scores of test borings into land formations. Largely as a result of these borings, the entire town of Valdez decided to relocate nearby rather than to rebuild on the old site.

The Army's response to urgent calls for disaster aid is not limited by geography or national borders; it renders assistance on a global basis. In 1962, when an earthquake devastated

Iran, killing some 10,000, injuring a like number, and rendering 25,000 Iranians homeless, the Army rushed in with hospitals, tentage, water purification units, field kitchens, and vehicles to save lives and alleviate suffering. Almost one year later, when a massive earthquake struck Yugoslavia, an entire Army hospital was airborne to the scene within hours.

Important as these peacetime roles of the U.S. Army undoubtedly are, the soldier himself knows that the Army is, first and foremost, a fighting force. His primary mission is to engage and subdue any ground force that initiates an aggression directed against his country. However, when the guns are silent and the engines of war tethered, the soldier still serves his country in many kinds of engagements on numerous unmartial battlefields. In many ways, his service off the battlefield is his finest hour.

III

Today's Army:
The View from the Field

The views of the Army of today differ according to the proximity or distance of the Pentagon. The farther the banks of the Potomac, the more the Army seems to become a purely military organism, devoted to military problems and seeking military solutions.

In the field, matters are stark, crisp, clearly defined. The exercise of command loses its Department of Defense delicacy, its overtones of subtle nuance, its undercurrents of compromise and accommodation. The troop unit commander in the field understands his authority; his orders are limited only by regulations, by good sense and professional judgment, and by the orders from *his* commander at the next higher echelon. As the mileage from Washington increases, the jargon changes, becomes more "GI" and less reminiscent of Harvard Business School and Johns Hopkins University. Organizational structure changes. The corporate format, the acronyms on which Washington thrives, fade. In the field, the "real army" emerges—the shooting, sweating, fighting army organized in the traditional companies, battalions, and divisions. In the way in which it is organized in the field is found the framework for its combat employment and the determinant of its tactics.

The generally accepted basic troop unit is the company (battery in the artillery, troop in the cavalry). Although it includes smaller formations, such as platoons and squads, the company is the smallest formation possessing a tactical and an administrative capacity. Like every troop unit in the Army, each company is manned, equipped, and organized in accordance with the applicable Table of Organization and Equipment (TOE) approved by the Department of the Army. The scope and complexity of modern warfare is reflected in the fact that in the Army there are now more than 500 different kinds of company-sized units, each formed in accordance with a specific TOE that has been designed to conform to the purpose of the unit. Companies vary greatly in size, but most have a personnel strength in the 175–200 range. Normally, a company is commanded by a captain.

Next in ascending order of size comes the battalion (squadron in the cavalry). It comprises a headquarters and two or more companies. If it is established as an integral part of a larger unit, the battalion usually has only tactical functions, with the administration being performed by the higher headquarters. If it operates as a separate unit, the battalion has both tactical and administrative responsibilities. The commander is usually a lieutenant colonel.

The regiment is both an administrative and a tactical unit. It consists of a headquarters and two or more battalions and is commanded by a colonel. The heyday of the regiment in the U.S. Army has passed. It is still an active formation, useful for some purposes, but its utility in current tactical groupings has diminished to the vanishing point.

Next in size is the brigade. Traditionally, the brigade has consisted of the headquarters and two or more regiments. Because the regiment has largely fallen into disuse in favor of the more maneuverable battalion, the brigade today includes battalions rather than regiments. A brigade is commonly commanded by a brigadier general, although many brigade-size units are commanded by colonels.

Above the brigade is the division. In modern practice, it is the smallest type of unit that includes elements of infantry, artillery, armor, and service troops as an integral part of its organization and that is capable of sustained combat operations, assuming normal logistical support. It is because of its combined-arms character and its combat endurance capability, that the division is the basic, major fighting unit. All armies reckon their combat capabilities in terms of the number of their divisions (as well as in terms of their quality). (Because an understanding of the nature and potential of the division is a prerequisite to understanding the tactical posture of the U.S. Army, the several kinds of divisions are explained below, immediately following a survey of the balance of tactical formations.)

The next larger unit above the division is the corps, consisting of a headquarters and a limited number of artillery, aviation, signal, engineer, and military police units, totaling in all some 3,000 officers and men. To this permanent nucleus is added whatever divisions and support troops the nature of the mission and the strength of the opposing force require. These augmentation units are not a permanent part of the corps; their numbers fluctuate with changes in the situation.

Normally, the corps performs little in the way of administrative functions, these duties being attended to at the next higher level. The corps mission is primarily combat. It is designed as a tactical formation for the execution of battle plans and for maneuver. The corps commander, ordinarily a lieutenant general, devotes only such attention to service support operations as is vital to the success of his combat mission.

The next higher unit, the field army, is an instrument of great flexibility, its size tailored to meet the demands of its responsibilities. It is characterized by self-sufficiency—a self-contained ability to discharge all of its tactical and administrative functions. The permanently assigned core around which a field army is built is relatively small, about 4,900 officers and men in all. They comprise the headquarters staff and specialized units directly supporting and servicing the headquarters. The corps and divisions allocated to a field army can bring its total strength to well over 150,000.

The field-army commander, who is either a lieutenant general or a full general, plans the over-all strategy and the broad tactical concepts for the corps and divisions he controls. On the eve of a campaign, he normally augments his corps with additional divisions drawn from his reserves, retaining in reserve a limited number for future deployment. As the battle progresses, he watches for opportunities to increase pressure on the enemy, and when he spots a critical point he moves in additional strength from his reserve force or by switching divisions from one corps to another.

During World War II, the U.S. Army introduced a new formation, which it utilized in the European Theater for the duration of the conflict—the army group. The necessity for the army group was created by the large number of field armies involved. So great was that number that for the theater commander to have dealt with them all directly on a continuing basis would have been cumbersome and impractical. Instead of this unworkable arrangement, he utilized the three army groups that were formed to close the gap between theater commander and field-army commander. The army group consisted of a headquarters, support and service troops, and a variable number of field armies, plus, as the occasion demanded, a number of corps and divisions not committed to a field army. The army group commander planned the general strategy and the large-scale tactical operations and controlled the execution of those operations by his subordinate units.

This seems the logical place to explain the Army's system of numbering major combat units. Divisions are identified by Arabic numerals followed by the type of division, as 29th Infantry Division. A corps is designated by Roman numerals, as XII Corps. Field armies are identified by a spelled-out number with the word "field" omitted, as Fifth Army. Army groups are also designated by spelled-out numbers.

One additional tactical formation is frequently employed—the task force. A task force is highly elastic; it fits no prescribed mold. In each instance, the task force is tailor-made to fit the pattern of the given mission and, normally, it ceases to exist when the mission is accomplished. The strength of a task force and the type of units it includes are determined by what is required of it and by what obstacles it is likely to face. The aim in forming a task force is to fashion an organization that is self-contained and equal to its mission without reinforcement. As employed in Army operations, the task force is highly mobile, boasts the maximum ratio of firepower to manpower, and drags the minimum logistical "tail" behind it.

World War I and the Square Division

Of all tactical units, it is the division—the fundamental, major combat unit—that merits closest examination. If the Army is a sword to be unsheathed in the nation's defense, then the division is its cutting edge. The division has existed in the U.S. Army for more than a century, but until World War I, when the square division was created, it did not possess its most significant characteristics: self-sufficiency and a combined-arms composition. The pioneer square division, the provisional 1st Expeditionary Division, was established in 1917. It was composed of a headquarters, two infantry brigades, a field artillery brigade, a machine gun battalion, an engineer regiment, a signal battalion, and support and service units. Each of the infantry brigades included two infantry regiments and one machine-gun battalion. Each of the infantry regiments consisted of three infantry battalions and one machine-gun company. The field artillery brigade consisted of two 3-inch field gun regiments and one 6-inch howitzer regiment.

The square division was able to mass great firepower and possessed great endurance in combat, but it was a ponderous organization. Its mountains of equipment and supplies and its seemingly endless personnel rosters—28,000 officers and men—made it unwieldy and difficult to control and maneuver. It was suited to the war for which it was created—a static war of mass formations with victory often going not to the swift but to the stubborn and the firmly entrenched—but the armistice that ended the war ended the era of static, mass warfare.

The advent of mechanization and improved weaponry after the war caused the U.S. Army to recognize that warfare of the future would place a premium on a more manageable, more maneuverable type of division. The planners began to consider a replacement for the square division.

The years that followed World War I were not kind to the Army; it was a time of belt-tightening and austerity. Military budgets were pared to the bone. Experimental divisional formations—and field-testing to prove them out—required funds that the Army simply didn't have. Turning to the best substitute, the Army conducted thorough, long-term, paper studies for a new divisional structure. By 1938, the studies had crystallized into a triangular division as a replacement for the square division.

World War II and the Triangular Division

In 1939, when the guns of World War II began to thunder in Europe and their echoes were heard in the United States, the Army was finally provided the means of putting the new concept to the test. In the large-scale 1940 maneuvers, five divisions field-tested the triangular format. The results were so satisfactory that nine divisions were triangularized before the year was out. Triangularization very soon followed for all divisions.

The triangular division lopped some 13,000 men from the old square-division strength, emerging with about 15,000. The reduction was achieved by reducing headquarters and administrative staffs and thinning out support and service troops. Equipment and matériel were cut to the essentials. The result was a lean, tough, more maneuverable division.

The offensive striking force of the triangular division consisted of three infantry regiments, three 105-mm. howitzer battalions, and one 155-mm. howitzer battalion. In support of these units were an engineer battalion, a medical battalion, a quartermaster battalion, a reconnaissance troop, a signal company, and a military police company. This mix of tactical units provided firepower sufficient to give punch on the offense and protection on the defense. And the streamlined configuration gave to the triangular division a mobility and a controllability the old square division never possessed.

World War II was a different war from the earlier world conflict. It was a war of movement, of evolving tactics, of mechanization, of vastly improved and even radically different weapons and devices, a war in which airspace became a new dimension of the battlefield. To meet the changing nature of land warfare, the Army experimented with variations of the division structure as the conflict progressed. From this emerged two new types of division: armored and airborne. Like the infantry division, they were organized on the basic triangular format. However, within that format, equipment, weaponry, and personnel strengths were adjusted to facilitate adherence to the different tactical employment for which each was designed.

The triangular division had proven itself in World War II and the Army saw little reason to tamper with it when the Korean conflict broke out. The only change of consequence was the addition of a tank battalion to the infantry division; this, plus minor adjustments in the strengths of divisional units, brought the division up to 17,752 men—a gain of some 2,500. The Army had not abandoned its long search for evolutionary improvement in the organization of the division, but the triangular format was highly satisfactory for the times, and so the search was not colored by an air of urgency. In 1955, the times changed abruptly; a need to accelerate the evolution appeared as a consequence of the Soviet detonation of an atomic weapon. The U.S. Army was no longer the only ground force with a nuclear capability, and it needed a division structure that would enable it to operate effectively in a combat environment in which atomic weapons could be turned against it.

Atomic Weapons and the Pentomic Division

What the Army sought was a division structure that permitted dual employment, either in conventional battle or in an atomic exchange. In a way, shaping a division for possible employment within an atomic context is a contradictory pursuit. On the one hand, the division must operate in a highly dispersed pattern and over a greatly enlarged area, because to maneuver in a mass formation is to present the enemy a tempting target for atomic attack. On the other hand, the division must be able to mass its firepower and its manpower to concentrate pressure in the offensive. The only method of reconciling these two opposing objectives is to improve weaponry in order to increase firepower, to enhance mobility to permit rapid concentration of strength and equally rapid dispersal, and to improve communications to enable commanders to maintain uninterrupted control over their dispersed, fast-moving units. Of the three types of triangular divisions in existence in 1955, only the armored division possessed an ability to sustain dispersed, mobile combat operations. To build this same kind of ability into infantry and airborne divisions, the Army created the pentomic division, and by 1958 all divisions had been reorganized on the new pattern.

Under the pentomic format, the three infantry regiments were replaced by five battle groups, a new tactical unit smaller than the regiment but larger than the battalion. The battle group was designed for sustained combat operations either alone or in combination with one or more of the other battle groups. Individual and crew-served weapons were replaced by improved models that increased firepower, decreased weight, and simplified operation and maintenance. The number of vehicles and heavy weapons in the airborne division was reduced sharply to provide a reasonably high degree of air transportability for the division; similar but less sweeping cuts in the infantry division made possible partial airlifts. Manpower of the airborne division was cut some 5,000, to 11,486. Not as deeply cut, the infantry division emerged with a strength of 13,748. Armored strength remained at 14,617, very close to what it had been in the triangular format.

Each of the three types of pentomic divisions included an artillery element. For the infantry, division artillery consisted of five direct support battalions—each with one 105-mm. howitzer battery and one 155-mm. howitzer battery—and one general support battalion consisting of one 8-inch howitzer battery and one rocket battery (Honest John). Artillery in the armored division comprised three 105-mm. howitzer batteries and one general support battalion consisting of two 155-mm. howitzer batteries, one 8-inch howitzer battery, and one Honest John rocket battery. In the airborne division the artillery was stripped down to five 105-mm. howitzer batteries and one Honest John battery.

The pentomic division was not intended to be a permanent or even a long-term solution. It was intended from the outset as a workable, interim measure to fit the division framework to the demands of both conventional and nuclear warfare. Meanwhile, the search for a better division structure continued.

One factor that Army planners meant to retain and to extend in the new division was the combat command format peculiar to the armored division. Both in its earlier triangular form and now in its pentomic configuration, the armored division included three so-called combat commands. They were nothing more than small, tactical headquarters to which the division commander could allocate any combination of the division's combat elements for an operation or a series of operations. The combat command provided the means of exercising control over the tactical units, and it gave the division commander a vital link for coordinating and maneuvering his combat elements. The combat command concept made for the kind of flexibility that is necessary on a modern battlefield without sacrificing the control that prevents a combat operation from deteriorating into a number of uncoordinated little actions. The combat command system was built into the new division concept that was developing rapidly.

ROAD

The new division, called ROAD (Reorganization Objective Army Division), was ready for trial in 1962. Two divisions were reorganized on the new pattern and were exhaustively field-tested. The "road tests" revealed a few minor pings in the engine, and they were deftly engineered out. By 1964, all divisions had been converted to the ROAD organization, and one new type—the mechanized division—was added to the roster to give the Army four distinct types of ROAD divisions: infantry, airborne, armored, and mechanized. (See Charts 1–4.) The new member of the team, capitalizing on mechanization, boasts a fleet of wheeled and tracked vehicles—many of them armored personnel carriers—to give it great ground mobility. It is a fast-moving pursuit and maneuver force, and its fundamental task, like that of the infantry, is conventional offense and defense: seizing and holding an area on the offense, and, on the defense, denying an area to the enemy. The infantry division has a greater capacity than the mechanized division for protracted combat in adverse weather and terrain. The airborne division is a rapid reaction, tactical force that is adapted to the battlefield's third dimension—air space. The airborne division is flown to the battle zone by Air Force craft assisted by the division's organic aircraft; the troops either parachute or are airplane-landed in a vertical thrust against the enemy. The armored division is the mailed fist that strikes hard, fast, and deep. Its punch comes from its tanks and other tracked and wheeled heavy vehicles, from its integrated, armor-protected weapons systems, and from its high degree of overland mobility.

All ROAD divisions have a common base. Although there are slight variations in the composition of the base, for all practical purposes it consists of the division headquarters, three subordinate brigade headquarters (thus retaining the triangular armored division's format of three combat commands), the division artillery, an engineer battalion, an aviation battalion, a signal battalion, a cavalry squadron, a military police company, and a support command. The primary mission of the cavalry squadron is reconnaissance; it perpetuates the term "cavalry" because it employs ground vehicles and aircraft in much the same manner as troopers of old employed horses.

The support command provides the division's medical, administrative, maintenance, and supply services. The division artillery (slightly reduced and modified for the airborne division) includes three 105-mm. howitzer battalions, a missile battalion equipped with Honest John and Little John rockets, and a composite battalion of 155-mm. and 8-inch howitzers. The Honest John and Little John rockets and the 8-inch and 155-mm. howitzers all possess a nuclear capability in addition to a conventional capability. Firepower, both nuclear and conventional, is greater in the ROAD division than it was in the pentomic organization.

The great feature of the ROAD division is its high degree of flexibility and versatility. This it owes to its three brigade headquarters and its maneuver battalions. (The battle group introduced in the pentomic division was abandoned in the ROAD division in favor of a return to the smaller battalion.) Within this framework, the division commander has the means to tailor a task force around each of the brigade headquarters. As the circumstances suggest and his judgment determines, he can allocate to a brigade any mix of maneuver battalions, artillery, engineers, and other support elements for a specific mission. If the circumstances alter, he is free to adjust the composition of each brigade task force by regrouping his units. ROAD divisions provide commanders the kind of flexibility and freedom they must have to cope with swiftly changing combat situations.

There is no rigid assignment of maneuver battalions to a ROAD division either by number or type. In each case, the allocation of the quantity and the type of maneuver battalions to a division is determined by its mission, by the terrain and environment, and by the strength and composition of the enemy. However, a representative allocation that would be considered normal in most cases would be for an infantry division, eight infantry and two armored battalions; for an airborne division, nine airborne infantry battalions and one armored battalion; for a mechanized division, seven mechanized infantry and three armored battalions; and for an armored division, six armored and five mechanized infantry battalions. Because there is flexibility in the assignment of maneuver battalions to a division, no division is forced into a prescribed organizational mold that is ill suited to the situation. For example, an infantry division employed in extremely poor tank country might have no assigned armored battalions, but the same infantry division fitted out for operations in prime tank terrain might gain as many as four or five armored battalions. Because the composition of a ROAD division can change, its strength is subject to fluctuation at various times. However, strength is usually just above the 15,000-man level for infantry, mechanized, and armored divisions, and around the 13,500 mark for an airborne division.

A completely new type of ROAD division—the airmobile division—emerged in mid-1965 with the activation of the 1st Cavalry Division (Airmobile) to meet the pressures of the war in Viet-Nam. (See Chart 5.) There were cogent reasons for creation of the new type of division, and all of them hinged on one of the major keys to modern land warfare: mobility. All ROAD divisions have some degree of mobility by air. The armored division, with its great weight of tanks and of wheeled and tracked weapons and equipment, is least adapted to air transport. The infantry and the mechanized divisions are a little better suited to an airlift. Much better adapted to air transport is the streamlined airborne division. But the new airmobile division possesses an inherent capacity for air transportability far exceeding that of the other four types of ROAD divisions. Its unprecedented ability to fly into combat is due, in large part, to its own built-in air-lift capability. The airmobile division possesses nearly 450 aircraft (all but 6 of them helicopters of 3 types), as compared to approximately 100 aircraft assigned to each of the other ROAD divisions. And the load that the airmobile division must transport has been dramatically lightened. For example, the almost 3,200 ground vehicles of the infantry division have been cut to some 1,600 in the airmobile division.

Because it is so "flyable" and because it can soar aloft on

its own wings, the airmobile division has given fresh meaning to mobility and maneuverability of ground units. It provides the Army with a whole new order of tactical options and responses—an ability to leapfrog the enemy, to land troops in intact units ready for immediate combat, to exploit a situation by instant shuttling of forces within a battle zone, to graduate the principle of surprise to a new level, to render rapid self-support by using organic aircraft for logistical purposes, to strike deep in the enemy's rear, and to withdraw rapidly. These are capabilities that are eminently suited to the fluidity of guerrilla warfare, as the 1st Cavalry demonstrated so quickly and effectively in Viet-Nam.

Like other types of ROAD divisions, the airmobile organization is built on a division base and a variable number of maneuver battalions. Approximately one-third of the men in the maneuver battalions are qualified paratroopers, thus enhancing the tactical versatility of the division. The airmobile base includes division headquarters, the three brigade headquarters, division artillery, a support command, an aviation group, an engineer battalion, an air cavalry squadron, a signal battalion, and a military police company. Division artillery comprises three 105-mm. howitzer battalions, an aerial artillery battalion, and an aviation battery. The support command includes a maintenance battalion (for other than aircraft), an aircraft maintenance and supply battalion, a supply and service battalion, and a medical battalion.

The ROAD concept is likely to remain valid for a long time to come—its longevity a result of its lack of rigidity. Three different types of ROAD divisions in combat in Viet-Nam—infantry, airmobile, and airborne—have proved well suited to the demands placed upon them. Within the elastic framework of the ROAD division, the Army planners can add, subtract, or alter units to place proper emphasis on new developments in weaponry, in matériel and equipment, and in tactics. The ROAD structure holds things together in a neat package, but it has "give" where it counts.

Chart 1
INFANTRY DIVISION (ROAD)

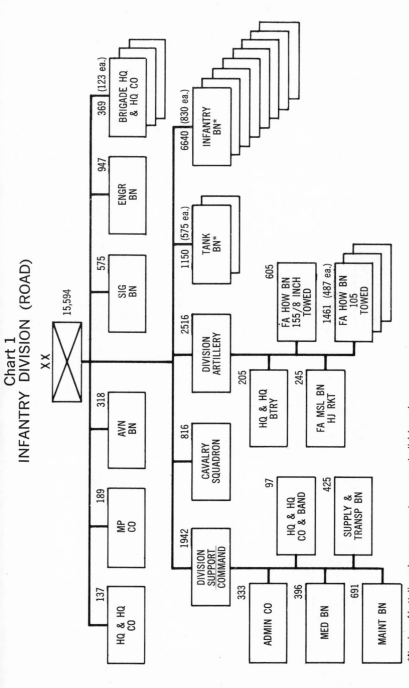

*Number of battalions shown represents an example division only.
Composition of divisions may vary.

Chart 2
AIRBORNE DIVISION (ROAD)

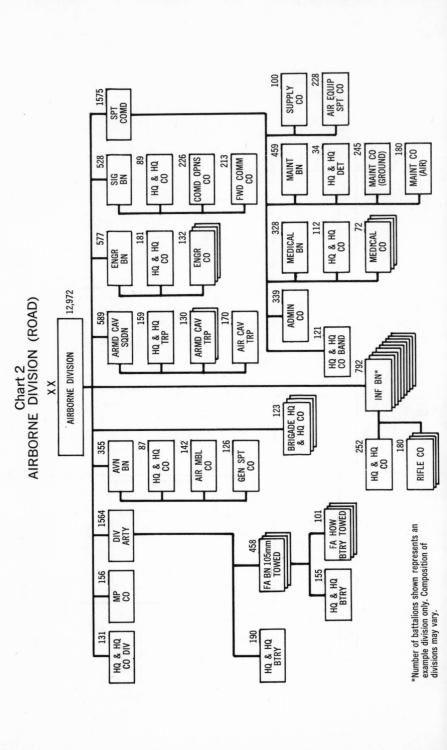

*Number of battalions shown represents an example division only. Composition of divisions may vary.

Chart 3
ARMORED DIVISION (ROAD)

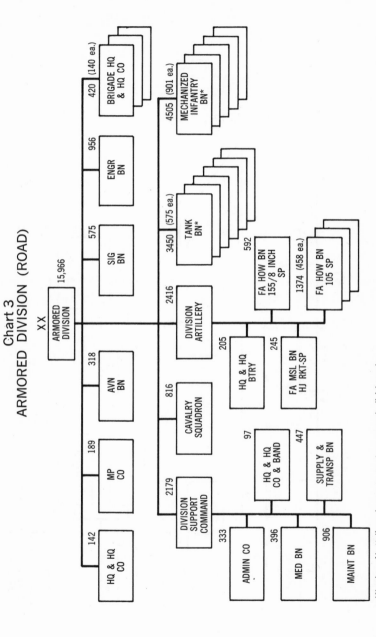

*Number of battalions shown represents an example division only. Composition of divisions may vary.

Chart 4
MECHANIZED DIVISION (ROAD)

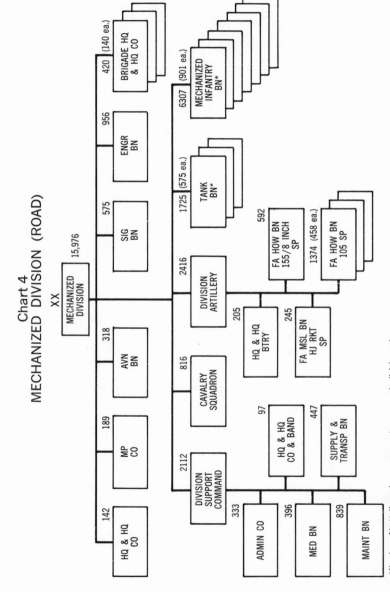

*Number of battalions shown represents an example division only. Composition of divisions may vary.

Chart 5
AIRMOBILE DIVISION (ROAD)

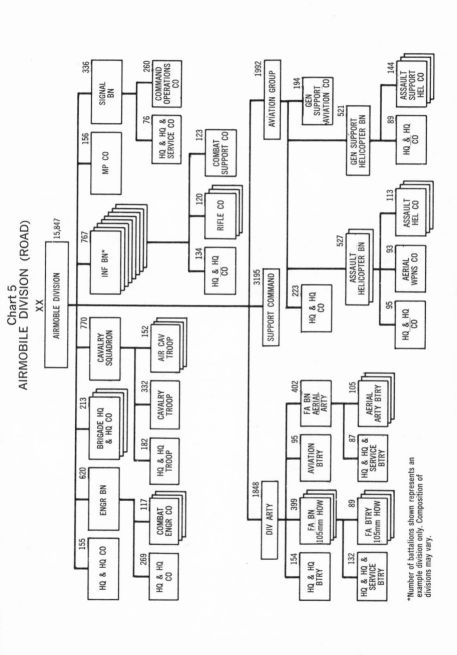

*Number of battalions shown represents an example division only. Composition of divisions may vary.

IV

Today's Army:
The View from the E-Ring

Who commands the U.S. Army?

The question is not trivial. Without an understanding of the system of command and control, there can be no meaningful understanding of the Army as an operational military entity or as an organ of government.

The President of the United States is the Commander in Chief of the Armed Forces. However, command of the Army does not stem directly from the White House. The route from commander to commanded is not quite that smooth and undiverted. Presidential power over the military is not absolute and unlimited. Under the American scheme of governmental checks and balances, the authority of the Commander in Chief is hedged and restricted by those powers that are reserved to the Congress and the Supreme Court.

Presidential authority over the Armed Forces originates in Article 2, Section 2, of the Constitution: "The President shall be Commander in Chief of the Army and of the Navy of the United States, and of the Militia of the several states, when called into the actual Service of the United States." That the framers of the Constitution saw fit to include this section in that fundamental charter of government is illuminating. By virtue of his authority over all segments of the executive branch, the President already enjoyed executive power over the military forces of the nation. The framers of the Constitution saw no need to include a special section declaring Presi-

48

dential supremacy over the State Department or the Treasury. Why, then, was the military singled out for special attention, and why was the office of Commander in Chief created to be occupied concurrently by the President? This Constitutional proviso was the Founding Fathers' effort to establish clearly the principle of civilian control over the military. They felt uneasy in the presence of standing armies, and they intended Article 2, Section 2, as a safeguard against the rise of a military dictatorship in the republic.

The Army, of course, predates both the Constitution and the man in the White House. A creature of the Continental Congress, the Continental Army was closely controlled by that body at the outset. But a political body in the throes of establishing a new nation and deficient in military experience cannot lead an army on the battlefield. Congress created the post of Commander in Chief of the Continental Army and entrusted it to George Washington. He leaned over backward to consult faithfully and fully with his political masters and to report to them regularly, never questioning the principle of civilian supremacy. And Washington was, after all, Washington —his prestige was unassailable, his character unimpeachable, his dedication unquestionable, his popularity unchallengeable. But to Europeans watching the drama unfolding on the American continent, he was also the personification of the new nation. Emissaries from abroad sought him out at least as often as they sought out the Congress. He was a heroic figure casting a heroic shadow—and Congress stood in that shadow. The Commander in Chief's pre-eminence, coupled with the delegates' ineptitude and indecision in dealing with military matters, caused Congressional influence over the Army to wane. Aware that the nation could scarcely expect to have a Washington always available to wield military power selflessly, the framers of the Constitution created the post of Commander in Chief to be occupied by the President—the one official who could not misuse military power as a lever to raise himself to higher office.

However, if the President as Commander in Chief could

not move upward, there was the chance that he could stay put, using his military resources as a means of entrenching himself in the nation's highest office and of assuming dictatorial powers for that office. To preclude such a possibility, Congress retained numerous controls over the military. Some were fundamental: appropriating the funds without which the Armed Forces could not function, fixing the strength of the military and prescribing the terms and conditions of enlistment, and retaining the exclusive right to declare war. Some Congressional controls, such as confirming all promotions to general officer rank, were relatively minor, although politically useful. Later, each chamber of Congress established a permanent Armed Forces committee to keep the military under continuous scrutiny.

The Evolution of Civilian Control

For today's Army, the second most important link in the chain of command is the Secretary of Defense, a civilian appointed by the President.

The genesis of the office of the Secretary of Defense goes back to Revolutionary days when the need for an executive agent to exercise civilian control of the military on a day-to-day basis was recognized. The first step in the evolution of the office was taken in 1776 when the Continental Congress designated five of its members to serve as a Board of War and Ordnance. Five years later, the delegates appointed a Secretary of War to succeed the Board. In 1789, when the new federal government came into being, Congress established the War Department as a Cabinet agency to administer military affairs under the authority and direction of the President—Commander in Chief. The Secretary of War exercised powers delegated by the Commander in Chief to enable him to function as the operating head of the military establishment.

Over the years, the authority and prestige of the Secretary of War waxed or waned according to the strength of purpose and determination of the incumbent and according to whether or not a "strong" or "weak" President occupied the White House. President James K. Polk, autocratic and independent, over-powered his Secretary of War and his generals; in particular, General Taylor discovered that his strategy in the Mexican War was being determined for him in the mansion at 1600 Pennsylvania Avenue. Taylor fumed and chafed and then, like another famous general in another war 100 years later, sought to bring pressure on the White House by "leaking" his story to the press. He was no more successful in this ploy than was General Douglas MacArthur in his well-publicized conflict with President Harry S. Truman during the Korean conflict. Perhaps more than any other occupant of the White House, Abraham Lincoln took charge of military strategy and opera-tions. In the year 1862 alone, without consulting his General in Chief, he organized the Army into four corps, created a western command, countermanded a deployment order to Gen-eral Irvin McDowell's corps, created the Army of Virginia, fired the Secretary of War, and played musical chairs with his generals.

The principle of civilian control over the military is too in-grained, too much a part of the fabric of American life, to be challenged seriously. But is it true, or merely glib, to say that war is too important to be entrusted to the generals? In the purely technical area of the prosecution of war, should the operational military decisions be made by political authorities or by those whose whole training and experience have been devoted to the accumulation of military expertise? This ques-tion has confronted and confounded generals, secretaries of war and of defense, and Presidents.

The problem of command of the Army became acute in the War of 1812, when civilian control of the military was inter-preted by the Congress to mean civilian command. The results were chaos and near disaster. Not until 1814 did Congress grant the Army a degree of freedom to get on with the war.

In 1821, an attempt to solve the problem of command of the Army within a purely military context was made by creating the office of General in Chief. The newly conceived General in Chief was to be the Army's "first soldier"—its operational commander. This concept acknowledged the pre-eminent Constitutional authority of the President as Commander in Chief and, also, the authority of the Secretary of War acting in the name of the Commander in Chief to exercise delegated responsibility for supervision of administrative and financial functions of the Army.

Unfortunately, the concept, so workable on paper, proved unsound in operation. A fundamental flaw was that the authority of the General in Chief was defined in vague terms, and his working relationship to the Secretary of War was not defined at all. The relationship between the two became a series of conflicts and a rivalry for power. Bypassing command channels, the Secretary frequently issued orders directly to officers in the field without so much as a "courtesy copy" to the commanding general. For his own part, the "first soldier" tended to regard the Secretary as a politician playing with little tin soldiers. At best, relations between the two were formal, strained, and unproductive.

The Impregnable Staff Bureaus

Despite the rivalry with the office of the Secretary of War, the office of General in Chief might have been tenable had it not been for the condition of the Army staff during the nineteenth century. At headquarters level, staff departments were charged with the function of rendering logistical and administrative support for the fighting man, each staff department being responsible for its segment of the total task. The trouble was that the departments had grown into ingrained, inbred, independent bureaus reporting directly to the Secretary of War. Each bureau was a separate island, and the only bridge to the mainland terminated in the Secretary's office. Bureau chiefs enjoyed life tenure and were noted for their longevity (one quartermaster general ruled for an incredible forty-two years). Under the circumstances, no bureau chief exhibited the slightest inclination to jeopardize the security of his citadel by recognizing the authority of the General in Chief as an echelon interposed between himself and the Secretary. Politically astute and jealous of their prerogatives, the bureau chiefs were determined to maintain their sinecures.

One General in Chief, William T. Sherman, was so hamstrung by War Department neglect and bureaucratic evasion that he appealed to President Ulysses S. Grant. Before entering the White House, Grant had himself occupied the post of General in Chief; but although he was fully acquainted with the absurdity of Sherman's situation, he offered no relief from it. Dismayed, Sherman temporarily removed his headquarters from Washington to St. Louis, thus making any solution of the problem even less likely.

Sherman's successor in office, General Philip H. Sheridan, fared no better in achieving command over the Army. His tenure was marked by a consistent and unsuccessful series of attempts to storm the stout defenses of the bureaus. Sheridan warned that the "multiple representation of the Commander in Chief in the persons of the several chiefs of bureaus of the War Department has been steadily opposed by all the eminent generals who have commanded armies in this country; . . . military operations cannot possibly be conducted with success under such a system of administration."

The next incumbent, General John M. Schofield, divided his problem into its two parts: his relationship to the Secretary and his relationship to the bureau chiefs. A man of vision and objectivity, he adopted as his fundamental policy vis-à-vis the Secretary a forthright and unequivocal recognition of the Secretary's pre-eminent authority. In his own words, Schofield observed that "under the government of the United States an actual military commander of the Army is not possible." In 1888, Schofield informed the Adjutant General that no order was to be issued on the General in Chief's behalf without the prior knowledge and approval of the Secretary. Thus, at long last, the rivalry between the commanding general and the Secretary ended. But if Schofield had eliminated the first part of his problem, he could do nothing to solve the vexing issue of the bureaus. The bureau chiefs had their walls too well guarded—and many Congressmen pulled guard duty.

Finally, in 1898, the Spanish-American War did what Schofield could not; it exposed the dangerous absurdity of the rigid compartmentalization and crippling impregnability of the bureaus—a system that, coupled with Congressional (and national) indifference, had left the Army without equipment, facilities, and properly trained, professional leaders. In addition, the Spanish-American War catapulted the United States into a position of prominence among the world powers, and led to a realization on the part of the government that now, more than ever, was a time for the country to have an army to match its role in world affairs.

The Root Reforms

President William McKinley appointed Elihu Root as Secretary of War in 1899. The appointment could not have been more felicitous. An incisive, logical thinker, trained in objective analysis by his legal experience, Root gathered facts with impartial deliberateness, seeking the basic causes of the mess he had inherited. He was struck by recurring evidence that the Army had never been permitted to discharge its primary obligation: to prepare itself intelligently and consistently in peacetime to cope with war. Always the preparation had come too late, following the outbreak of war instead of preceding it.

Root recommended the replacement of the uncoordinated and independent bureaus by a general staff system adapted from the German model. He urged the clear definition of the relationship between the commanding general and the Secretary of War on the one hand and the commanding general and the staff on the other hand, the establishment of an Army War College and a system of higher military education for the officer corps, the revision of the criteria for officer promotion to de-emphasize advancement based on seniority, the initiation of large-scale troop maneuvers, the stockpiling of reserves of arms and equipment, and the preparation of contingency plans for use in any possible conflict. Root had done his homework well; his was a masterful blueprint for reconstructing the Army into a modern, coordinated, and effective force.

But a blueprint is one thing; persuading the carpenters to follow it is quite another. Root knew that the framing of his program and the passage by Congress of enabling legislation were widely separated. He set out on a campaign to facilitate the second step. On an extensive speaking tour, he appeared before influential groups across the country, eloquently outlining a portion of his plan here, another portion there. Each portion was bite-size, not enough to choke his audience but enough for them to chew on. He couched his remarks in convincing logic and buttressed them with undeniable facts and figures. Every address concluded with a tactful yet emphatic appeal for assistance in influencing the Congress to grant its approval of his plans.

Predictably, there was a chorus of opposition, but Root was determined and kept plugging away. Time—and Root's own calm, methodical, irrefutable logic—worked in his favor. His first concrete success came in 1901 when Congress authorized establishment of the Army War College. In 1903 came his grandest success: Congressional enactment of the General Staff Bill. Under the new law, the office of the commanding general was abolished; in its place was created a military Chief of Staff to supervise all Army forces, both line and staff, under the direction of the President and the Secretary of War. The existing staff bureaus were brought together under the collective title of the Special Staff, and were placed under the jurisdiction of the Chief of Staff; thus, reporting directly to the Secretary had become a thing of the past. A new entity, the General Staff, was charged with the formulation of plans that would create in the Army a state of combat readiness equal to the demands of any contingency and with advising the Chief of Staff of the most effective ways to enhance military capability in peacetime and to employ that capability in wartime.

The new law was among the most important legislative packages related to the military ever promulgated by Congress. For the first time in history, the Army possessed a defined chain of command under the over-all principle of civilian control of the military. At the same time, it provided the Army with its first authorization and structure for rational planning for the national defense. Refinement, adjustment, even profound change still lay in the Army's future, but with passage of the General Staff Bill the U.S. Army received its charter as a professionally conceived fighting force.

The system of command and control of the Army today retains the basic format laid down in the 1903 legislation. At the apex is the President in his role as Commander in Chief (but sensitive to Congress, with its power to appropriate funds and to legislate on military matters, and to the Supreme Court, with its power to declare his decisions unconstitutional). Just below the Commander in Chief is the Secretary of Defense, a post created by the National Security Act of 1947, the so-called Unification of Armed Forces Act that established the Department of Defense, the Joint Chiefs of Staff, and the Department of the Air Force. The Commander in Chief's principal deputy, the Secretary of Defense, speaks in his name and, on his behalf, exercises over-all, day-to-day supervision of the entire military complex. On the next lower level of the ladder are two rungs. One is occupied by the Joint Chiefs of Staff, through whom operational control of the combat forces is exercised. The second rung is occupied by the Secretary of the Army (the changed designation of the former Secretary of War), and by the Secretaries of the Navy and the Air Force, each of them responsible for supervision of the internal affairs of his department. Within the Army, the Chief of Staff is the principal adviser to his service Secretary. He is accountable to the Secretary for the level of performance of the Army and for the state of readiness of troop units to meet any contingency. Under the direction of the Secretary, he heads all members and organizations of the Army.

It is perhaps symbolic that most of the generals assigned to

Army Departmental Headquarters in the Pentagon occupy offices in the E-ring, the outermost of the five concentric corridors that make up the building and, hence, the only one boasting windows that look on the outside world. Though there may be a solitary die-hard here and there, by and large the generals have adopted the larger view that their outside windows symbolize. They are realists who have come to grips with the fundamental questions of command, accepting civilian supremacy unquestioningly and recognizing that "command authority" is derivative and is limited.

Who commands the Army? The truth is that there is no solitary, all-powerful commander responsible only to himself—not even the Commander in Chief—unless one adopts the position that under an elective form of government, with ultimate power residing in the ballot box, it is the people who command.

The Army Staff System

The Chief of Staff's responsibility is crushing—accountable as he is for the level of performance and the degree of combat readiness of all of the men and units of the Army. Obviously, he cannot hope to accomplish his mission unless he has available and instantly responsive to his needs a large, well-organized, and smoothly functioning staff to supplement his eyes and ears, to serve as specialists in technical areas, to sift through and refine the myriad of details, to study the problems and suggest appropriate solutions, to serve him as a "think factory." On every level, commanders have staff officers to advise and counsel within their areas of competence, but on the Chief's level the ability and the vision of the staff is a matter of gravest importance because there is no "upstairs" within the Army proper to turn to.

Often, a staff officer's lot is not a happy one. Working under great pressure and keenly aware that his recommendations will shape the nature of the decisions adopted, he recognizes that, to the uninformed, he is frequently a mere "desk jockey." Yet without the desk jockeys, there could be no race.

The Army staff system dates back to the Revolutionary War, when the Continental Army instituted a staff closely paralleling the British model. Its function then, as until the beginning of the twentieth century, was largely confined to administrative and technical matters—paying, feeding, and housing the troops; procuring and distributing arms and equipment; providing transportation, communications, medical facilities, and all of the similar supporting services. Nowhere was there provision for strategic planning, for thinking ahead of the war that might come and for preparing to meet it successfully. The commander was expected to be his own strategic planner if, indeed, any consideration was to be given to the need to plan for the future. But if he were to devote himself both to exercising day-to-day direction of the Army and to strategic planning, he would necessarily have to skimp on one or the other. Institution of a General Staff under the 1903 legislation plugged this dangerous gap. The Army now had its full-time planners to look into the future and to advise on the best means of meeting it.

This did not eliminate or even diminish the need for the Special Staff—the technical and administrative services. The quartermaster, the surgeon, the adjutant, the engineer, the provost marshal, and the other staff specialists did not magically become surplus to the Army's needs once the General Staff came on the scene. Their services were just as vital as before; more so, in fact, as military affairs continued to grow increasingly complex and technical. But the General Staff provided the framework within which the activities of the specialists could be coordinated and made to conform to the broad strategic concepts they were evolving.

Staff organization has been far from static in the twentieth century, as the Army continued to grope for perfection. The objectives of this sustained refinement of the Army Staff have been several. One aim has been to eliminate duplication of effort and to promote economy. Another purpose has been to remove from staff sections the vestiges of command functions that properly are the province of commanders and not of advisers. (But some staff officers are *both* advisers and commanders; the surgeon, for example, advises on medical matters and also commands the medical personnel and their activities.) A third objective, especially in recent years, has been to inject the concept whereby sections of the Special Staff having related and compatible functions are grouped under the over-all management of the appropriate section of the General Staff. A further aim has been to restructure the Army Staff to provide better means of keeping pace with the rapid rate of technological advances.

The most recent major reorganization of the Army staff was undertaken in 1962. The manifold purposes of the reorganization, known as Project 80, were conservation of money and manpower, elimination of the fragmenting of responsibilities and resources, simplification and strengthening of the channels of command and control, and delegation to lower echelons of those functions not required to be performed at departmental level. The reorganization was approaching midway point in its introduction when the Cuban missile crisis of 1963 intruded, creating an urgency and a tenseness that could easily have halted the changes in progress. To its credit, the Army did not revert to the earlier system that—despite admitted shortcomings—boasted the advantages of familiarity, but instead accelerated the changes even as it coped with the crisis. The Cuban problem put the new system tó a stern test while it was being introduced and before it had become entrenched, demonstrated the essential soundness of the system, and suggested improvements that could be incorporated while the reorganization was taking place.

Since Project 80, there have been other modifications introduced into the Army Staff, though none has been so all-embracing as the 1962 revisions. Unquestionably, there will be additional modifications in the future. Today, the top echelon of the Army wears a new face. The General Staff has expanded, the Special Staff has contracted, and new major Army com-

Chart 6
ORGANIZATION OF THE DEPARTMENT OF THE ARMY

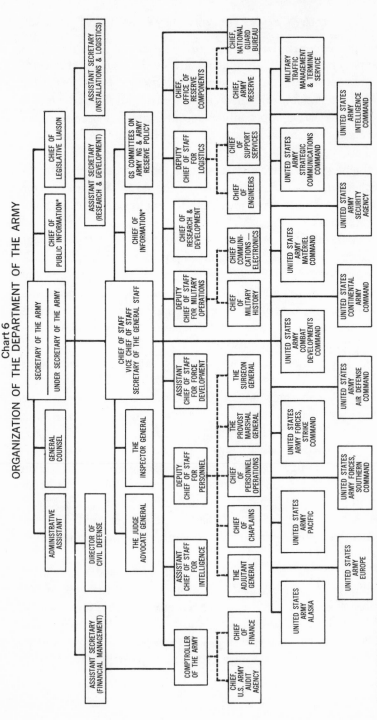

*The Chief of Public Information also serves as Chief of Information.

mands have been created. Although the changes have been extensive, their true significance is conceptual rather than physical. They represent the crystallization of a military philosophy that had been developing slowly—perhaps too slowly. To appreciate the significance of what has happened, it is necessary to examine more closely the structure at the top.

In its latest form, the major elements of the General Staff serving the Chief of Staff include the Deputy Chief of Staff for Personnel, the Deputy Chief of Staff for Military Operations, the Deputy Chief of Staff for Logistics, the Assistant Chief of Staff for Intelligence, the Assistant Chief of Staff for Force Development, the Chief of Research and Development, the Chief of the Office of Reserve Components, and the Comptroller of the Army. (See Chart 6.) Basically, the Deputy Chief of Staff for Military Operations (DCSOPS) is the Army's strategist for joint operations employing the resources of the Armed forces as a whole. His fundamental job is to plan the Army's role in joint operations, to ascertain the character and strength of the Army forces that will be required to carry out that role, and to determine how currently available, combat-ready Army units can best be utilized in pursuit of that strategic mission. The Assistant Chief of Staff for Force Development (ACSFOR) is closely linked in his responsibilities to those of DCSOPS. The prime difference is that DCSOPS is concerned with joint operations, whereas ACSFOR concentrates on unilateral operations involving only Army troops. As a matter of fact, until ACSFOR came into being in the spring of 1963, DCSOPS had been charged with planning for the employment of Army forces in all types of operations, joint and unilateral. Fear that the pressure of joint planning might cause work on unilateral operations to be neglected led to shrinking the DCSOPS mission to joint operations and to creating ACSFOR to handle unilateral planning.

Even so, ACSFOR must temper his parochialism with suitable consideration for the Army's role in joint operations as conceived by DCSOPS. ACSFOR is obliged to plan the type of Army force structure that will provide a maximum of balanced units, operationally ready for unilateral employment, consistent with requirements outlined by DCSOPS for joint operations, and within the money and manpower limitations imposed on the Army.

In keeping with the principle of grouping appropriate members of the Special Staff under suitable members of the General Staff in the interests of cohesive, effective management, DCSOPS exercises jurisdiction over the Chief of Communications–Electronics and the Chief of Military History. The Chief of Communications–Electronics will sound more familiar by his pre-1962 title, Chief Signal Officer. (The change in title signified other changes that are discussed later in this chapter.)

The Deputy Chief of Staff for Personnel is charged with the formulation of Army-wide personnel policies and with general supervision of the over-all personnel management programs and procedures throughout the Army establishment. He is responsible for manpower procurement; directly operates the Reserve Officers Training Corps program; and coordinates and controls the administrative, morale, protective, and spiritual activities related to the Army's manpower. Operating under his policy control are the Chief of Personnel Operations, the Adjutant General, the Surgeon General, the Provost Marshal General, and the Chief of Chaplains.

The Deputy Chief of Staff for Logistics (DCSLOG) is the Chief of Staff's principal adviser on matériel matters. He plans and oversees the Army's industrial purchasing, contracting, and procurement activities; develops logistic doctrine, policies, and procedures; and conceives and coordinates the supply system. DCSLOG exercises staff supervision over the Chief of Engineers and the Chief of Support Services (a new title created when the office of the Quartermaster General was abolished in the 1962 reorganization).

The Assistant Chief of Staff for Intelligence (ACSI) is responsible for planning and coordinating the various efforts and activities related to fulfillment of the Army's intelligence and counterintelligence requirements. ACSI formulates doctrine and operational concepts pertaining to intelligence activities and promulgates measures for the safeguarding of classified data. A major responsibility of ACSI is supervision and coordination of the Army's surveillance and reconnaissance efforts to secure timely, accurate information of enemy troops—their dispositions, weapons emplacements, lines of communications, and movements. For these purposes, a highly sophisticated array of devices and techniques are employed, among them unmanned aerial drones, advanced radar and infrared devices, long-range photography, exotic sensors, and automatic data processing.

The Chief of Research and Development is charged with the planning, coordinating, and supervising of the Army's numerous research and development operations and projects. The ultimate objective of the activities over which he exercises staff supervision is the development of superior equipment, weaponry, matériel, and technical procedures. To this end, all of the basic sciences are utilized as avenues for exploration. Formerly, each of the technical services of the Army Staff had a fairly free hand in conducting its own R&D programs, with a minimum of centralized control. But scientific breakthroughs cannot be compartmentalized to conform to staff divisions. Television, to take one example, has a potential for military employment for communication, training, battlefield surveillance, meteorological observation, artillery fire-control, and psychological warfare. With such diverse application of the fruits of accelerating scientific accomplishment increasing constantly, there is real danger in an organization as vast as the Army that the left hand won't know what the right hand is doing—which means duplication, missed opportunities, waste, and lack of maximum exploitation. Establishment of the office of the Chief of Research and Development was meant to rule out such possibilities or, at the very least, sharply diminish the likelihood of their occurrence.

The Chief of the Office of Reserve Components is the principal adviser to the Chief of Staff on matters related to Reserve affairs. He is the over-all supervisor of all plans, policies, and procedures affecting the Army National Guard and the Army Reserve. Responsive to him are the Chief of the National Guard Bureau and the Chief of the Army Reserve. Because of a statutory provision, zealously supported by the individual states, the Chief of the National Guard Bureau is also permitted direct access to the Chief of Staff without reference to the Chief of the Office of Reserve Components. The principle of good management would be better served if this dual channel for the National Guard were not perpetuated.

The Comptroller of the Army, of all the members of the General Staff, is in a unique position: He serves two masters. Like other officers of the General Staff, he is responsible to the Chief of Staff. However, he is also directly responsible to the Office of the Secretary of the Army, and his activities are supervised by that office. The Comptroller is the uniformed financial manager and "efficiency expert" of the Army. He conceives, coordinates, and oversees the Army's accounting, budgetary, fiscal, statistical, and management engineering operations. Under his jurisdiction are two members of the Army Special Staff: the Chief of Finance and the Chief of the U.S. Army Audit Agency.

Completing the staff at departmental level are three divisions that perform specialized functions for the Army's "first soldier." The Judge Advocate General is the Chief of Staff's principal legal adviser; the Inspector General acts as his eyes and ears, evaluating the state of training, effectiveness, readiness, and morale of the units and agencies of the Army; and the Chief of Information is his official spokesman.

The Major Commands

As a result of Project 80 and of other studies since 1962, a number of new major commands have been established to join those already in existence. (See Chart 6.) Seven of the Army's major commands are of interest at this point because, while they are not part of the staff, they are an integral part of departmental headquarters; like the Army Staff, they operate under the direct supervision of the Chief of Staff. Furthermore, they are charged with responsibilities that until quite recently were largely assigned to the Army Staff. In fact, some of the major commands were created specifically for the purpose of relieving segments of the Army Staff of many of their duties. They include the U.S. Continental Army Command, U.S. Army Combat Developments Command, U.S. Army Matériel Command, U.S. Army Security Agency, U.S. Army Strategic Communications Command, U.S. Army Intelligence Command, and Military Traffic Management and Terminal Service. (The six additional major commands—U.S. Army Alaska; U.S. Army Europe; U.S. Army Pacific; U.S. Army Forces, Southern Command; U.S. Army Forces, Strike Command; and U.S. Army Air Defense Command—are troop commands that operate in a joint framework with counterpart commands of the other services. They are examined in detail in Chapter IX.)

The U.S. Continental Army Command (CONARC) is a complex agency as well as a large one. It is the principal, all-inclusive, domestic troop command and, as such, it exercises general supervision over the five armies in the United States and over the Military District of Washington. At the same time, CONARC has a second fundamental mission, training.

To appreciate the complexity of the training mission it is necessary to digress sufficiently to consider the Army branch system. All military personnel are assigned to a branch of the Army that is organized for a specialized function. Some of the branches, called "arms," are designed for fighting or for direct, close support of a combat unit; these arms are Infantry, Artillery, Armor, Corps of Engineers, and Signal Corps. The remaining branches, called "services," render supporting and/or administrative services to the Army as a whole. Some branches have a dual mission as both arms and services and are identified both ways. The services are Adjutant General's Corps, Corps of Engineers, Finance Corps, Quartermaster Corps, Army Medical Service, Chaplains' Corps, Judge Advocate

General's Corps, Ordnance Corps, Signal Corps, Chemical Corps, Military Police Corps, Women's Army Corps, Transportation Corps, and Army Intelligence and Security Branch. Prior to 1962, CONARC's training responsibility extended only to the arms. The training within each of the services was planned, controlled, and supervised by the member of the Army Staff whose area of responsibility included the special functions of that service. Thus, the Army had not one but a number of training systems and, among them all, the staff operated a score of training centers and service schools.

Project 80 put an end to this duplication of facilities and resources and fragmentation of responsibility by consolidating most training and all service schools under the authority of CONARC. Blanketed under this centralization was the Army National Guard and the Army Reserve. CONARC's mission embraces both individual and unit training.

Consolidation of training has made possible a streamlining of curricula and courses, a reduction in training time, and a drastic decrease in duplication. For example, six supply courses formerly taught at five different service schools have been compressed into a single course taught at a single school. Another example is the case of Fort Gordon, Georgia, where the Southeastern Signal School, the Military Police School, and the Civil Affairs School had been operating as three separate activities, each with its own overhead and its individually formulated curriculum. Under its over-all training authority, CONARC has combined all three into one Army School Training Center, functioning under a single overhead organization.

The U.S. Army Combat Developments Command (CDC) consolidates into one activity and under one commander the functions that had been shared by several members of the Army Staff, by CONARC, and by other Army agencies. These functions include the development of organizational and operational doctrine; the development of matériel objectives and standards consistent with that doctrine (but not production and procurement of matériel itself); and field testing, "wargaming," and executing cost effectiveness studies of all the foregoing. The broad mission is to formulate current operational concepts for the Army in the field and, anticipating future changes in the character of land warfare, to determine how the Army will have to be organized, equipped, and employed to achieve victory in future combat environments. CDC's conceptual planning ranges by five-year increments to a target date at least twenty-five years ahead. It has, either completed or in preparation, blueprints for the desired combat posture of the Army in 1970, 1975, 1980, 1985, and 1990. And already, some thought is being devoted to the combat characteristics envisioned for the Army beyond the 1990 timeframe. Thus, CDC provides a comprehensive, forward-looking, and continuing approach to a unified combat doctrine throughout the Army.

As a result of the recommendations embodied in Project 80, the Army Matériel Command (AMC) was established as a logical companion to CDC and CONARC, forming a triumvirate that directly affects the stance of the soldier in the field. CDC is the testing ground where ideas for improving the tactics and the equipment of the soldier are proven out. CONARC is the training ground where the soldier is schooled and practiced in the military skills. AMC is the arsenal where weapons, equipment, and matériel of every description are developed, procured, and maintained, and from which they are distributed to the soldier and his unit. All three agencies have a close and continuous interdependence. Implicit in the interrelated activities of these three commands is a direct involvement in the Army's research and development programs—CDC determining developmental goals, AMC performing R&D to meet these goals, and CONARC conducting personnel training programs to create an ability to use the fruits of the R&D projects effectively.*

* As noted earlier, all Army R&D (in addition to AMC, the Surgeon General, the Chief of Engineers, the Army Security Agency, and other Army activities perform specialized R&D) is programed, coordinated, and supervised by the Office of the Chief of Research and Development.

The internal pattern of AMC reveals seven subcommands. Five of these subordinate agencies—the Electronics, Missile, Mobility, Munitions, and Weapons commands—are commodity oriented; that is, they are designed to cope with a family of related end-items. The remaining two subcommands —the Supply and Maintenance Command and the Test and Evaluation Command—support the servicing activities. Some of the advantages of AMC's commodity-oriented format became readily apparent by considering what has happened to one prime commodity—ammunition. The Munitions Command provides continuous supervision and control over all ammunition—conventional, chemical, biological, radiological, and nuclear—from development through production and procurement to supply, distribution, and maintenance. Prior to this "single manager" policy, responsibility for ammunition was divided among the Chief of Ordnance, the Chief Chemical Officer, and others. What is true of ammunition is likewise true of the rest of the Army's hardware. Thus, the 1962 reorganization substituted an integrated logistics system under a single commander for several systems under diverse controls. The result has been to furnish the Army one basic source for all matériel and one primary controller for the entire supply system.

One of the newest major commands, established in 1964, is the Strategic Communications Command (STRATCOM). It directs, controls, and operates all of the Army's strategic telecommunications facilities—radio, wire, and cable. STRATCOM also incorporates into its operations portions of the overseas commanders' long-lines (long-distance telephone) networks. Prior to creation of STRATCOM, the Army's strategic communications were commanded by the Chief Signal Officer. When his command was transferred to the new agency, the Chief Signal Officer was redesignated the Chief of Communications–Electronics, charged with conceiving and developing plans, policies, and doctrine for tactical and strategic employment of communications, and especially with integrating into the communications systems such exotic electronic advances as satellite relay techniques. A major effort of the Chief of Communications–Electronics is geared to development of improved tactical communication devices and techniques.

Of even more recent vintage is the U.S. Army Intelligence Command (USAINTC), established in February, 1965. USAINTC shares its stock in trade with the U.S. Army Security Agency (ASA), but the two separate intelligence agencies have different purposes and functions. With a primary mission embracing all Army counterintelligence activities within the continental United States, USAINTC controls the consolidated counterintelligence units that formerly had been under the direct supervision of either CONARC or ACSI. All background investigations of Army personnel, both military and civilian, are conducted by USAINTC. The Army Security Agency's mission is suggested by the terms jocularly applied to it: the "big ear" and the "electronic snooper." Relying on highly sophisticated and vastly complex electronic equipment and devices, ASA's special forte is long-range eavesdropping and, turning the coin over, utilization of electronic countermeasures to defeat attempts to listen in on our communications systems.

The Military Traffic Management and Terminal Service (MTMTS), also dating from February, 1965, assumed functions that previously had been assigned to the Chief of Transportation and other agencies. MTMTS is the single manager for all of the Armed Forces for surface transportation of military cargo and passengers within the United States and is the operator of all military ocean terminals except those maintained by the U.S. Navy for support of the fleet. In effect, establishment of MTMTS completed allocation of sole responsibility to each of the Armed Forces for transportation in the medium in which it is at home—the Navy's Military Sea Transportation Service on the water, the Air Force's Military Airlift Command in the air, and the Army's Military Traffic Management and Terminal Services on land.

After 1962, it became inevitable that some of the traditional members of the Army Staff would disappear into the Army's historical files. Training functions had been consolidated under CONARC, matériel procurement under AMC, combat development under CDC, basic research and development under the Chief of R&D, and so on. Stripped of so many of their duties, several segments of the staff were left with little justification for continued existence. Project 80 had not only anticipated this situation but also had sought consciously to precipitate it. The change made good sense from a management point of view. Eliminated from the staff were the offices of the Chief of Ordnance and the Chief Chemical Officer. The Chief of Transportation was transformed into a planning directorate within the Office of the Deputy Chief of Staff for Logistics. The Quartermaster General was replaced by a Chief of Support Services with drastically reduced duties and resources. Transformation of the Chief Signal Officer into the Chief of Communications—Electronics has already been noted.

However, it must be emphasized that it was only the *offices* of the chiefs, with all their overhead, that were eliminated or realigned. Ordnance, chemical, transportation, signal, and quartermaster remain unaffected as *branches* of the Army. Nothing has occurred, nor is likely to occur, that abolishes or even reduces the Army's vital need for officers and men functioning in these specialized fields.

Project 80 completed what was begun by the 1903 legislation establishing the Army's authority for creation of a General Staff. The result is a thoroughly overhauled, modernized departmental organization that has excised vestiges of an antiquated, contradictory, wasteful, and cumbersome system. Members of the Army Staff are now—as they should have been all along—solely planners and advisers to the Chief of Staff. Today, the General Staff performs the role envisaged for it in 1903: development of strategic plans and formulation of Army-wide concepts and policies designed to achieve a posture of combat readiness. Command-like, operational duties once fragmented among the staff have been properly consolidated in the major commands. New major commands have been created along "functionalized" lines conforming to mission and capability, thus casting off the strait-jacket of the old and rigid Special Staff compartmentalization. As the appearance of new techniques and devices reveal the possibilities, even more "functionalization" can be expected in the future.

The clear delineation that has been created between the functions and responsibilities of the Army's departmental structure and combat elements has not—as some pessimists predicted—divorced Pentagon planners from the realities of the battlefield. All sections of the Army Staff maintain close and constant liaison with the operational units to insure realistic and rapid reaction to the needs of the combat elements. For example, from the beginning of U.S. involvement in South Viet-Nam, the Army Staff has been represented in the area by the Army Concept Team in Viet-Nam (ACTIV). By direct observation of combat operations, monitoring after-action reports, and day-to-day association with the troop units, ACTIV has evaluated Army concepts, doctrine, matériel, and weaponry to ferret out ways of enhancing combat effectiveness. ACTIV recommendations led to arming helicopters for delivery of suppressive fire, development of new types of body armor for combat troops, introduction of improved cargo and fuel handling equipment, and a number of other important advances.

The Army's struggle to create a responsible and responsive staff system seems finally to have succeeded.

V

The Quick and the Deadly

Lieutenant General Nathan B. Forrest may have been weak in his grammar when he observed that victory went to the one who "got thar fustest with the mostest," but nobody can fault him on his grasp of military science. As long ago as the era of Caesar's legions, military men realized that in land warfare the tune is called by the quick and deadly—the force that is the most mobile and that can bring to bear the greatest firepower. The only change since Caesar's day is that now the quick are quicker, the deadly deadlier.

Mobility is the ability to move a force fast enough and far enough to achieve a specific strategic or tactical purpose, regardless of terrain, climate, or enemy obstacles. But mobility alone has no real meaning in combat unless it is teamed up with firepower. When mobility has achieved its purpose by delivering a fighting force to a target area, firepower imposes the will of the attacking force.

Modern warfare demands of an army that it possess an extremely high order of mobility and firepower. In addition, the commander must have a wide range of choices. One mission may be best served by a slow approach. Another may require a lightning thrust and a heavy barrage. An army must possess the kind of maneuverability and weaponry that permit selectivity to fit the situation.

Military mobility has two faces: strategic and tactical. Strategically, it is the capacity for movement of a force from its base to an objective area in accordance with a strategic plan.

The U.S. Army's strategic mobility is provided by the Air Force and the Navy, as well as by its own internal resources. Tactically, mobility is the ability to maneuver effectively on the battlefield. The Army provides its own tactical maneuverability, depending on organic wheeled, tracked, amphibious, and aerial vehicles.

Truly modern tactical mobility dates from the Nazi introduction of its *blitzkrieg* forces in World War II. *Blitzkrieg* tactics were based on three elements: breakthrough, rapid and deep penetration, and envelopment and destruction of enemy units. Often, Nazi ground forces were provided "vertical artillery" support by aerial dive-bombers. *Blitzkreig* tacticians originated the "vertical envelopment" in 1940, when they parachuted a specially trained force into battle—the first actual combat employment of airborne troops. *Blitzkrieg* won battles for the Nazis, but ultimately it was a major factor in losing the war for them because it awakened the Allies to the full significance and the potential of modern mobility. In the forefront of the drive for ground maneuverability was the U.S. Army. The result was its creation of massive armored and airborne forces, and the enhanced mechanization and maneuverability of the infantry and supporting services. Allied ground forces made bold and effective use of amphibious attack, of vertical envelopment, of armored thrust, of mobile infantry tactics—and in the end beat the Nazis at their own game.

In Korea, where the difficulty of the terrain and the nature of the conflict ruled out *blitzkrieg* tactics on anything more than a limited scale, the Army introduced a new vehicle for providing maneuverability to combat and supporting forces—the helicopter. With the jungle fighting in Viet-Nam, the helicopter became a key factor in mobility.

For some years, the Army has been exhibiting commendable restlessness in trying to conquer the time and space factors of the battlefield. The continuing search for better means of moving men, weapons, and matériel faster, farther, more easily, and more safely has borne some interesting fruit; still more is ripening at the Army's test and development centers. Wheeled vehicles now come in a wide variety ranging from a low-silhouette, jeep-sized cargo and ammunition carrier (in which the driver either sits aboard or walks crouching along the side) to the giant BARC, a transporter for tanks and outsized cargo that swims ashore and then rolls to the combat area. In between are articulated trucks, double-jointed vehicles that tilt in two directions at once to clamber over the roughest terrain; rolling liquid transporters whose huge tires are also fuel tanks; and assorted vehicles that are undaunted by the greatest extremes of climate that exist on earth. There are tracked vehicles that can float themselves across water barriers, and others that can cross watercourses completely submerged to a depth of over 20 feet. One adaptation of the M-48 tank carries a folded, steel bridge atop; when it reaches a water barrier or crevasse it unfolds and launches the bridge into place hydraulically, leaving a 60-foot span sturdy enough to carry heavy-duty traffic over the obstacle. Tracked personnel carriers with bodies of hardened aluminum are faster and farther-ranging than ever before and are readily air-transportable. The Army's newest helicopters fly faster, carry heavier loads, and provide better protection for crew and passengers. One twin-engined model, the CH-37, can lift a 7,000 pound load for 180 nautical miles via an external sling.

Today, organic aviation within ground units has added a new dimension to the overland and overwater mobility of the soldier. With his rotors, his wheels and tracks, his amphibious vehicles, and the sturdy boots that are his initial mobility equipment, the soldier can strike more targets more readily over a wider area than ever before. And he can strike harder because firepower had made the same sort of strides as mobility.

Firepower—the total ability of a force to hurl bullets, shells, missiles, or other projectiles against a target—was a sleeping giant for centuries after the Chinese developed the crude gunpowder that eventually made firearms possible. The giant showed the first stirrings of life when an ancient, anonymous inventor thought to pour gunpowder into a deep iron tube, to place a round stone atop the powder, and to insert a red-hot wire through a small touch-hole in the base of the tube. The resulting explosion hurled the stone (and, occasionally, bystanders) through the air. With that rough cannon as a point of departure, weaponry commenced, developing slowly for some centuries and accelerating sharply around the eighteenth century. Since then, weaponry developments have been so many and so revolutionary that only a sampling can be given here: rifling of cannon bores to increase accuracy and range, shaping of projectiles, recoil mechanisms to absorb the shock of discharge, breech loading to simplify and hasten loading, smokeless powder, fused shells for delayed detonation, the machine gun, automatic fire, fragmentation grenades and shells. There is almost no end to the list. Especially during the twentieth century, weaponry developments have been radical. Two stand out as exerting a profound influence on warfare: effective rocketry and atomic devices, the former because it tremendously increased the range and speed of a projectile, and the latter because it greatly intensified the potential for devastation. Together, they introduced a wholly new scale for assessment of firepower and have created a new set of combat tactics.

But rockets, missiles, and atomic warheads tend to obscure the true meaning of firepower. Firepower is more than a matter of making the biggest "bang"; it is a matter of providing a commander with a variable "bang"—an arsenal of weapons of different characteristics and of graduated deadliness—to enable him to tailor his firepower to the needs of his mission. He employs artillery against an enemy bunker dug into a facing hillside, but against an enemy dug in on the reverse side of the same hill he uses mortars that can arch over the crest and come down at a sharp angle. Against a tank he uses armor-piercing shells, but against a personnel concentration he uses a high-explosive shell. Rifles, machine guns, and grenades are lethal in close combat, but they are a waste of time against an enemy who is two or three miles down the road.

To be meaningful, firepower must provide an entire range of lethal instruments. Effective firepower is selective firepower.

In tailoring its firepower to the requirements of modern land warfare, the Army has been moving in several directions simultaneously. One seemingly paradoxical trend has been simplification of weapons systems that continually grow more complex. The goal of simplification has been pursued from the point of view of the soldier in the field who uses and maintains the arsenal. Weapons have been made lighter wherever possible, automatic features have been engineered into the design, subassemblies have been made interchangeable in "families" of weapons, caliber options not vital have been eliminated, weapons have been "ruggedized" and "weather-proofed" to enhance reliability, more accurate sighting devices have been incorporated, and simpler maintenance techniques have been devised. A part of this effort has been concentrated on making one weapon do the job that used to require two or three. An example is the SPIW (special-purpose individual weapon) now under development; it combines the pin-point target capability of a rifle with the dispersed target capability of a grenade launcher.

Another trend in ordnance (the collective term for the Army's weapons) has been a progressive increase in maneuverability, range, and accuracy of the heavy weapons. Self-propelled weapons have been made more reliable, their armor has been strengthened, and the ratio of range and speed to weight has been improved. Amphibious weapons have been made more amphibious, and many previously land-locked weapons have had an amphibian capability engineered into them; a similar program has been conducted with respect to air-transportability.

In its work on conventional ammunition, the Army has sought to improve what it has and to develop completely new types. There have been successes in both areas. Ballistic variations between different lots of the same type of ammunition have been curtailed sharply. Every category of ammunition has had smoke and flash properties suppressed. An imaginative development has been the duplex cartridge for 7.62-mm. rifles and machine guns. The duplex is a piggy-back affair of a standard casing housing two bullets, one snuggled behind the other. The forward and trailing bullets each have a slightly different aerodynamic configuration so that when they leave the muzzle they follow divergent flight paths. At a distance of 100 yards, the two bullets travel about 11 inches apart, thus diminishing to a great extent the chance of a missed target. A further development has been the creation of a family of extremely high velocity projectiles that are eminently effective in bringing down rapidly moving, distant targets.

In the atomic field, the Army has had to consider two parts of the problem: the warhead and the delivery system. As far as the warheads are concerned, the objectives have been to develop both the implosion and thermonuclear types, to make them "clean" (minimize their radioactive fallout), to reduce their size and weight, and to produce warheads providing a wide range of yields. In delivery systems, the objectives have been to insure tactical flexibility by building an atomic-delivery capability into a variety of weapons systems and to engineer into each a high order of safety and reliability. Atomic-delivery characteristics are now shared by most of the missiles and rockets and by a number of the tubed artillery pieces. One of the most interesting in the last category is the M-28, which demonstrates the vast progress that has been achieved in reducing the size of atomic warheads and in improving the flexibility of the delivery systems. The M-28, popularly known as the "Davy Crockett," is a 120-mm. recoilless rifle that is normally mounted in a jeep, from which it fires its atomic warhead. However, it is readily demountable, and three soldiers can hand-carry the gun plus a warhead a short distance and fire it from the ground.

The aim of the Army's rocketry efforts has been to attain greater simplicity, mobility, reliability, and adaptability. The consequence has been the appearance of a well-populated "family" of operational rockets and missiles. Two of them, the 66-mm. rocket and the colorfully christened Redeye, have been squeezed into the individual soldier's knapsack, so to speak. The 66-mm. rocket, a four-and-a-half-pound lightweight, is fired from the shoulder and is effective against tanks and armored vehicles. With his Redeye guided missile, which is also shoulder-fired, a soldier can knock a low-flying plane out of the air; his missile "homes in" on the heat of the plane's engine and flies up the "tail pipe." Some of the other operational missiles and rockets include Hawk, Nike-Hercules, Sergeant, Pershing, and the two Johns: Honest and Little. Honest John and Little John are both mobile, solid-propellent rockets; the former, 27 feet long, has a range of about 23 miles, while the latter is slightly less than half as long and has a range of about 15 miles. Sergeant is a fully mobile guided missile with a 135-mile range. Pershing, air-transportable and mobile on the ground, is a two-stage guided missile with a 400-mile range. Hawk and Hercules are both mobile surface-to-air guided missiles. Hawk is intended primarily for battlefield air defense; Hercules, effective against high-flying aircraft and air-breathing missiles, is intended primarily for defense of populated areas and key installations.

The Army has still other rockets and missiles in various stages of development. One that is close to achieving operational status is Chaparral, a surface-to-air system intended for defense of forward tactical units against all types of aircraft flying at low-to-medium altitudes. The Chaparral system maintains four Sidewinder missiles at a time, in ready-to-fire condition from simple launch rails. For full-tracked, cross-country mobility, the Chaparral is mounted on a modified M-548 vehicle; for ordinary highway mobility it can be mounted on a trailer or it can be dismounted for static emplacement. A second missile system under development is the SAM-D, a surface-to-air missile system designed as a defense against high-performance aircraft and against short-range tactical ballistic missiles. Because of these design capabilities, it is intended principally for the defense of Army forces in the field. It might also be well employed in the continental United States as a terminal defense system.

Importance of Communications

The effect of all the significant advances in firepower and mobility has been to give the Army a combat potency greater than it has ever had previously. Assuming leadership that is professionally competent, incisive, and bold without being foolhardy, there is one more imperative if the full combat potential is to be realized: good communications. In their day, a runner, a signal flag, or a carrier pigeon sufficed to satisfy communications needs. Today's communications system must match the realities of modern land warfare.

It is now normal for a division to maneuver over an area that is two or three times larger than the sector covered by a World War II division; one company operates over an area that used to be the province of two or three companies. In Viet-Nam, with no front or rear in the conventional sense, the average ratio of square yardage to soldier increased some 600 times over what it was during the American Civil War. Not only has battlefield distance multiplied, but the tempo of war, influenced by the advances of firepower and mobility, has quickened spectacularly. These changes have intensified the difficulty of controlling and maneuvering forces, while at the same time they have placed an even higher premium on uninterrupted control and instantly responsive maneuver. The key to such maneuvering is communications resources. They must be instantaneous, flexible, continuous, and reliable. They must incorporate a capacity for long ranges and for high-volume, multiple usage. Components must be as small, as light, as durable, and as interchangeable as ingenuity can devise. Redundancy must be built into the equipment so that if one portion of the system is knocked out, a commander will not be left "speechless" and his command left directionless. Effective communications must exist on all levels on the battlefield, linking each unit with its higher, lower, lateral, and supporting units, and all of them must be interwoven into nets for immediate, two-way contact.

These are some of the factors borne in mind in redesigning and improving Army communications techniques and devices. Today, communications equipment that would have been considered unrealistically visionary as late as World War II is in routine use. Disregarding the sophistication of the equipment, merely the statistics alone make heady reading—a typical division maintains 180 or more separate networks for communicating, and it utilizes over 2,000 radios, plus field telephones by the hundreds and teletypewriters by the dozens. To all of that must be added the division's switchboards, radio relay terminals, and other components.

The technique that furnishes much of the information communicated is battlefield surveillance. The function of surveillance is to obtain from the battlefield data on the enemy's disposition and movements. Without such data, the commander cannot make the wisest, most effective use of his manpower and matériel resources. To keep the battlefield under surveillance, the Army employs visual observation, infrared, radar, and photographic techniques, both on the ground and in the air.

The most flexible of the techniques is visual observation performed either by fixed spotting and listening posts or by roving patrols. To extend the observer's capabilities, he is provided various devices to magnify objects and to enable him to see in the dark. An infrared image metascope weighing only 2 pounds permits him to read maps in darkness, to see 50 feet down a dark road, and to detect enemy infrared light sources 10 miles distant. Another aid enables him to drive at normal speeds at night without using his headlights. Undergoing terminal testing is a 10-pound radar with a 1-mile range—the first radar that can be carried and operated easily by a single soldier.

In the Army's inventory is a 115-pound radar that can detect moving figures at more than 4,000 yards and moving vehicles at 6,500 yards. A larger model extends the range to

5,500 yards and 20,000 yards respectively; it depicts the target on a television screen and indicates it by a sound signal. Still more sophisticated and more discriminating radars are in the works. High on the list of exotic devices is a laser range finder that enables an observer to determine rapidly the precise location of a target, thus increasing the probability of a first-round artillery hit.

For airborne battlefield surveillance, the Army utilizes both manned and unmanned craft. The unpiloted craft, radio-controlled drones, are equipped with especially sensitive cameras that take day or night pictures. The piloted craft are twin turbo-prop Mohawks outfitted with infrared sensors and photographic, side-looking radar.

The chapter that follows gives a representative sampling of the combat hardware developed in the mid-twentieth century and discusses the problems involved in getting matériel—and the men who use it—to the battlefield.

VI

Logic and Logistics

The dictionary fails utterly when it defines logistics as "The branch of military science concerned with the mathematics of transportation and supply, and the movement of bodies of troops." What a monumental display of lexicographic deficiency! It is like defining human reproduction as that branch of biological science concerned with the mathematics of population.

Army Regulation 320-5 does a better job. It defines logistics as "In its most comprehensive sense, those aspects of military operations which deal with: (1) design and development, acquisition, storage, movement, distribution, maintenance, evacuation, and disposition of matériel; (2) movement, evacuation, and hospitalization of personnel; (3) acquisition or construction, maintenance, operation, and disposition of facilities; and (4) acquisition or furnishing of services. It comprises both the planning, including determination of requirements, and implementation." But even AR 320-5 might well have emphasized the importance of logistics by pointing out that the success of an army as an effective fighting force rests on a tripod whose legs are strategy, tactics, and logistics. If one of the three legs buckles, the entire tripod tumbles.

In fairness, it must be admitted that the dictionary's inadequate definition, conjuring up as it does an image of a logistician with an abacus, is not far off the mark in suggesting the arrested level of efficiency in the Army's logistical system until fairly recent times. Prior to the entrance of the United States into World War I, Army logistics was almost exclusively the province of five members of the Army Staff: the Surgeon General, the Chief of Engineers, the Quartermaster General, the Chief Signal Officer, and the Chief of Ordnance. Each member of the quintet operated independently of the others, and virtually independently of the rest of the Army. In fact, each considered the others competitors and, in contracting for supplies for the Army, they actually bid against each other. By the time World War I had concluded, a start had been made in bringing order and logic into this chaos. It was only a start.

The eve of Pearl Harbor found the Army with logistical centralization of a sort. It is true that there were no less than fourteen different Army agencies directly involved in logistics, but all were subject to central supervision, control, and coordination. The flaw was that the Army provided not one, but two, central controllers: the Office of the Under Secretary of War and the Supply Division of the General Staff. The General Staff was responsible for determination of requirements and for distribution of matériel. The Under Secretary was responsible for the gap between those two functions—actually procuring the goods. The two controlling agencies were on speaking terms, but hardly more. Coordination and cooperation were more the exception than the rule. Thus, there was often conflict between what was needed by the Army (a General Staff responsibility) and what was obtained (the Under Secretary's bailiwick).

Altogether, the state of Army logistics in 1941 was deplorable. Item: Only seven of the Army's thirty-four under-strength divisions could have been completely equipped for immediate overseas deployment, and then only by stripping the remaining divisions. Item: The entire defense armament on Canton Island, a small but strategically important Pacific atoll, consisted of some fifty pistols and rifles in the hands of a single platoon. Item: The Corps of Engineers possessed no airplane landing mats—not one square foot—although wartime requirements eventually reached the grand total of 883 million square feet.

In March, 1942, President Franklin D. Roosevelt issued an executive order that reshuffled the War Department. Among other things, the order created the Army Service Forces as one of the coequal major commands; the other two were the Army Ground Forces and the Army Air Forces. (Initially, Army Service Forces was called the Services of Supply, quickly abbreviated to S.O.S.—an unintended but accurate summation of the situation.) Establishment of Army Service Forces marked the first unequivocal recognition of logistics as a fundamental factor in the prosecution of ground warfare and the first appearance of a single commander in whom was lodged Army-wide logistics responsibility. The new command absorbed the large staffs of the Supply Division of the General Staff and of the Under Secretary, and assumed the operational direction of more than forty Army agencies, depots, ports of embarkation, and other logistical activities that previously had functioned in splendid isolation under the over-all jurisdiction of the Chief of Staff. One flaw of the earlier system was retained in the new command—Army Service Forces served two masters: the Chief of Staff on all matters other than procurement and the Under Secretary of War on procurement questions. In practical terms, although this was not good management, it was no longer the grave handicap it had been, because the Under Secretary was now a procurement "watchdog" rather than a procurement "operator."

Army Service Forces was faced with an enormously complicated problem of overwhelming urgency. It had to expand all logistical operations tremendously and at breakneck speed, while at the same time it had to transform this hydra-headed monster into a controllable, coordinated entity. It had to procure staggering quantities of hundreds of thousands of items required to arm, equip, support, and sustain the men already in the Army and those arriving in a flood from draft boards, all of this at a time when sources of supply were disrupted by the war. It had to embark on a massive effort to engineer improvements into the equipment, devices, and weapons even as they moved down the assembly lines. Almost overnight, it had to build centers, training camps, depots, warehouses, bases, and fixed facilities of every description. It had to create global supply lines and ensure that they were fed an unceasing flow of matériel. It had to transport millions of soldiers to the dispersed battle zones and evacuate and hospitalize the wounded. All of these things, and more, the new command had to accomplish within a framework for which there were no precedents. No organization in the world—military or civilian, governmental or private—had ever before tackled a task of like scope and complexity. That Army Service Forces succeeded is a matter of record and a source of wonder.

From the experience of World War II came, at long last, a full appreciation of the proper role of logistics in modern warfare and a determination to prevent a return to old habits. In 1954, the Office of the Deputy Chief of Staff for Logistics was established with direct responsibility to the Chief of Staff for planning, programing, and budgeting all Army logistics and for formulating the Army-wide concepts and doctrine. In 1962, the Army Matériel Command was created with direct responsibility to the Chief of Staff for command and control of all Army-wide logistical operations. The system passed another milestone in 1965 when the same organizational principles that culminated in the establishment of DCSLOG and AMC prompted initiation of the Field Army Support Command (FASCOM).

Until the innovation of FASCOM, supply and supporting services within a field army operated vertically along a number of parallel lines—all separate. That is, support within the field army was channeled through seven different networks reaching from field army to division. Each network handled a different category of supplies and services: chemical, engineer, medical, ordnance, quartermaster, signal, or transportation. Each network was commanded by a different field-army staff officer who was, thus, in the contradictory position of simultaneously being a staff adviser to the army commander and also a commander in his own right. The field-army commander found himself with ultimate responsibility for seven separate channels of command in addition to his tactical command channel; and the division commander found himself forced to secure his supporting services from seven different sources. FASCOM eliminates these obvious shortcomings by relieving the field-army staff of command authority, by furnishing a single support commander directly under the field-army commander, by embacing the seven separate service support systems and converting them into a coordinated and functionalized field-army system, by introducing consolidated and computerized stock control and stock management, by furnishing the divisions virtual "one-stop shopping" service, and by providing a unified, consolidated operation that is more rapidly and more flexibly reactive to change in the tactical situation.

Today, Army logisticians must support, supply, and maintain the most widely deployed military force on earth. It is a military force that operates in every terrain and environmental condition, that must possess a capability for conventional or for nuclear response, that is engaged in hot war, cold war, and lukewarm nibbling at one and the same time. To meet these multiple requirements, the logisticians have adopted multiple approaches.

One approach is the letting of "educational" contracts to industry. Satisfaction of the procurement needs of the Army is dependent upon the productive capacity of the nation's industrial complex. Industry turns out goods in response to demand. Two hundred million Americans represent an enormous demand for refrigerators, so industry maintains an enormous capacity for producing refrigerators. How many hand grenades do these 200 million Americans shop for? If the Army ceased procuring hand grenades because it had, for the moment, reached desirable stock levels, grenade plants would shut down and the productive capacity would dissipate. To prevent a situation that could prove tragic in an emergency, the Army keeps a very close check on industrial capabilities and, whenever

advisable, supplements its normal procurement with "educational" orders to keep critical manufacturing know-how and
facilities from rusting away. So-called educational contracting
is especially important in creating capacity to produce a new
military item for which there is little immediate demand but
that would be needed in quantity if conditions altered.

A vital military necessity in today's fast-paced world is the
ability to mass a tactical force in a distant spot in an extremely
brief period. This can be accomplished by airlift, as has been
amply demonstrated. But such a force, if it is to be of more
than transitory effectiveness, must have supporting equipment
and matériel beyond the capacity of the airlift for simultaneous
delivery. The supporting services and supply items must be
readily available in order to permit the force to sustain itself in
combat pending the creation of supply lines. The logisticians
have produced an answer to this puzzle by conceiving the principle of prepositioning. In several strategic overseas areas, carefully balanced stocks of arms, ammunition, combat vehicles,
equipment, and other supplies are maintained in instantly usable
condition for immediate issue in the event a tactical force
should be airlifted into the region. Although not a perfect solution, inasmuch as stocks cannot be prepositioned everywhere
at the sovereign will of the United States alone, it is a sound,
partial solution that makes possible a quick-reaction airlift of
combat forces to many potential hot spots. An imaginative var-
iation of this scheme is the prepositioning of forward floating
depots in friendly ports abroad. Each floating depot consists of
a small flotilla of Victory ships whose holds are loaded with
combat-support vehicles, weapons, equipment, and matériel
protected by humidity plants installed aboard. The ships can
discharge their cargoes directly ashore or can steam to another
port more accessible to an airlifted force.

Miniaturization and standardization are two approaches to
the same objectives: lightening the logistical load and simplifying the job of the soldier in the field. By miniaturizing wherever feasible and by utilizing lighter-weight materials, logistics

experts are making an inch do the job of a foot, an ounce replace a pound. The results have been startlingly successful in reducing size and weight with no sacrifice of operational characteristics. Indeed, in most instances the new-look items are both Lilliputian and more effective.

The logisticians are relentless in their efforts to upgrade the effectiveness of every item that the Army uses, and they are demonstrating an ability to plow fresh ground, not merely to dig familiar furrows a little deeper. One example is their development of a small, infrared weapon sight that enables a gunner to locate a distant target at night and to aim his weapon accurately. Another is a truck that unrolls its own steel-matting road before it from a giant cylinder carried on the truck bed, thus enabling the vehicle to drive over an otherwise impassable area and to leave behind a roadway for following vehicles. Still another is a collapsible, helicopter-transportable hospital, complete with operating room, laboratory, independent power source, plumbing, and temperature and humidity controls. Within thirty minutes after delivery at the site, the hospital is fully operational, its inflatable walls automatically pumped up to form a twenty-bed patient ward.

One bit of fresh ground the Army logistics experts have been cultivating involves the highly sophisticated fuel cell, a radical device wherein fuels are converted directly to electric power, completely eliminating the wasteful heat cycle of gasoline and Diesel engines. The implications of this process are sweeping. Because the system has the potential ability of converting fuels into ten times as much usable power as conventional engines, the Army's staggering fuel requirements could be relieved without jeopardizing its power needs. Because the system would operate silently, unlike ordinary power plants, it could be utilized near the enemy without revealing its location. And because the fuel cell is so efficient and compact, it could be developed into a vehicular power plant with the potential of enabling a vehicle to drive long distances, perhaps as much as 150 miles, on a single gallon of fuel.

Keeping pace with modern electronic wizardry, the Army logistics system has become one of the world's leading users of electronic data processing, employing computers for everything from determining how many size 11 jungle boots to procure to determining the trajectory of an experimental rocket.

This sustained drive to transform elephants into gazelles covers all of the more than 1 million separate items in the Army's inventory. Look at what has happened to the centrifugal pumps used in engineering operations. Until recently, more than a dozen different sizes of pumps were required to provide an adequate range of pumping capacity. By redesigning the operating characteristics, the Army has succeeded in whittling the total down to just four models, each of them with at least 85 per cent of their parts interchangeable, and all of them more reliable, more easily maintained, lighter, smaller, and cheaper than the numerous models they replaced. One of the new pumps, Mil-P-52469, is 75 per cent lighter and 80 per cent smaller than the model it succeeds.

Equally dramatic is the shrinkage of the 7-pound "Handie-Talkie" transmitter-receiver used by front-line troops for battlefield communication. A new set intended as a replacement consists of a 9-ounce receiver that clips on the helmet and a 15-ounce, hand-held transmitter that can be stowed in a pocket when not in use. The new transmitter-receiver operates on any one of 100 frequencies, is unaffected by intense heat, cold, or humidity, and is extremely rugged and weatherproof.

Computerization has introduced into logistics an entirely new degree of flexibility, reliability, and speed; it has reduced dependence upon human memory and compressed hours and days into seconds. Some of the computer applications have been unusually inventive. Take, for instance, the Army's brand-new computerized "mechanic," a footlocker-sized electronic device that can determine the cause of malfunction of military wheeled vehicles accurately in less than five minutes. The operator feeds into the computer brief information on the vehicle type, the engine number, and the difficulty. In minutes, the device types out in plain language a description of the cause, a list of the parts needed to remedy the breakdown, the stock numbers of the parts, and the specific sections of the repair manual that cover the necessary installation instructions. The device does everything except hand the repairman his tools.

Another "gee-whiz" electronic item plugs into any Army radio to convert Morse code dots and dashes into English letters appearing on a miniature screen, permitting any soldier unfamiliar with the code to receive the coded message when adverse atmospherics rule out intelligible voice communication. At 1½ by 2⅞ by 2⅞ inches, the device is, in effect, the world's smallest electronic computer.

As the marvels of every size devised for every purpose testify, Army logistics today has both the type of organization and the quality of thinking that survival in modern warfare demands.

VII

Strategy and the Army

The perfect military strategist is the one who will never receive acclaim for the wars he has won nor condemnation for those he has lost. The ideal strategy achieves its goal with no necessity to resort to war. The ultimate, the maximum aim of strategists is to attain bloodless victory. That aim is predicated on the assumption that if the strategy creates a military posture so impregnable and so undefeatable that any armed attempt to oppose it is foredoomed to failure, the enemy will have no rational alternative to keeping his guns holstered. This supreme objective is seldom reached because the human equation is an inextricable part of the military equation. The men who conceive the strategy, the men who are charged with execution of it, and the men against whom it has been designed and who, in turn, are framing their counter-strategy, are all subject to the errors and miscalculations of fallible humanity, and frequently the outcome, as history attests, is armed conflict.

When the primary aim of strategy is not achieved and the issue erupts into a clash of arms, the second responsibility of the strategist comes into play: to assure the greatest probability of successful prosecution and victorious termination of the hostilities. The over-all plans, the troop and weapons deployments, the meshing of the parts of the warmaking machinery into a comprehensive whole—all are ingredients of strategy. The battlefield execution of the operational plans constitutes the tactics. There is a gray area where strategy and tactics meet, an overlap that makes it difficult to say with finality where one ends and the other begins.

Military strategy does not exist in a vacuum, aloof and alone. It is part of a larger scheme of things—the national strategy. In its broadest sense, the national strategy is the process of development and employment of all the resources of the nation in support of the government's policies. Thus, it is an amalgam of all of the elements of national strength—military, political, economic, scientific, psychological, sociological—each framing its special strategy, sensitive to the needs and potentials of the other elements and responsive to the overriding national goal. Not in every situation is the same degree of prominence attached to each of the elements, but there is an inescapable interaction and interdependence of all the strategies that, in total, constitute the national strategy. Nowhere has this been illustrated better or more emphatically than in the American commitment in Viet-Nam, where extremely close coordination and mutual support among the military, political, economic, psychological, and sociological efforts were early harmonized into a "team" approach to the common goal.

In shaping strategy, military leaders must consider the aspirations of their own nation and those of the enemy or potential enemy. To be effective, military strategy must provide maximum promotion of one's own aspirations and maximum deterrence of any that may be in conflict. Several limiting factors determine the general pattern of military strategy. One series of limitations is imposed by the defense policies of the nation. Currently, these policies dictate that the United States will not launch the initial attack that marks the opening of an armed conflict; that the military response to an attack will be confined to the minimum degree of force consistent with the nature and scope of the attack; that the regular establishment, supported by an input from the draft, will be utilized, with mobilization of the reserves to be undertaken only if the regular establishment is inadequate to the need; that the military resources of the nation will be coordinated with the military resources of friendly nations in a mutually supporting system of alliances; and that the U.S. Armed Forces are subject to uninterrupted civilian command and control, whether or not war occurs. Another series of limitations upon the strategy is imposed by pertinent physical realities: the budget granted to the military, the manpower ceilings imposed, the level of U.S. technological sophistication, and the capacity of the industrial complex to produce the arms, equipment, and matériel desired.

What becomes apparent from all of the foregoing factors is that military strategists are subject to a welter of restraints and must accommodate their planning to these influences. It might appear that, if the United States were less principled and more militaristic, the task of the strategists would be eased. But, as a matter of fact, the very limitations under which U.S. strategy is formulated impart a certain strength to it, in two respects. First, the limitations make it clear to other nations that the United States has no aggressive aims, that it disavows the option of initiating "preventive" war, and that, as proof of peaceful intentions, it is prepared to absorb the first blow. Second, the limitations make U.S. strategy realistic and supportable and, therefore, fully credible to potential enemies. They cannot hope that a test of arms would reveal a strategy inconsistent with other aims of national life.

The Communist Threat

For more than a generation, American military strategy has been directed toward the containment and neutralization of the persistent threat posed by aggressive Communism. Throughout this period, the United States and other free nations have been challenged persistently by Communist expansionism originating in Moscow and Peking. The gravity of the threat is implicit in the Communist goal of world domination and in their amply demonstrated belief that the end justifies the means, with any device or expedient acceptable if it promises progress toward the Communist world system. The nature of the threat is equally clear. It is aggressive, global, flexible, persistent. Communist strategy embraces political, economic, psychological, and military attack—actual or threatened—at all levels of intensity.

The military strength of the Communist bloc is a trident,

whose three prongs are nuclear striking power, conventional capability, and unconventional forces.

At present, the nuclear striking power is built completely around the capability of the Soviet Union. The first successful detonation of a Red Chinese nuclear device on October 16, 1964, followed by subsequent detonations in 1965 and in 1966, underscored the atomic threat but did not materially alter its focus. In testimony before the Senate Subcommittee on Department of Defense Appropriations in early 1966, Secretary of Defense McNamara declared that the Chinese "could possibly develop and deploy a small force of ICBM's by the mid to latter part of the 1970's." The Russians possess both warhead and delivery systems in quantity and variety, deliverable on target by land-based missile, by submarine-launched missile, or by manned bomber. The Soviet Army is estimated to have on hand at least 180 intercontinental ballistic missiles with a range of 5,000 miles or more. These are supplemented by perhaps as many as 1,000 intermediate-range ballistic missiles available for targets up to 2,000-plus miles from the launch site. The Russians also have an undersea fleet of some 450 submarines, almost one-eighth of them nuclear-powered. About 10 per cent of the submarine fleet is equipped to launch relatively short-range ballistic missiles from a surfaced position. The Russians are believed to have made substantial progress in perfecting a long-range, underwater missile similar to the Polaris system. For manned delivery of atomic weapons, they have some 250 heavy bombers capable of a round-trip mission to almost any U.S. mainland target. An additional 1,400 medium bombers have a nuclear delivery capability at ranges slightly in excess of 2,000 miles.

Conventional capability—the second prong of the trident—is inescapably obvious and completely credible. It derives from the massive armies of the Soviet Union and Red China, plus the armies of the satellite nations. The military strength of the Russians and the Chinese is vested primarily in armies. This is consistent with the position of each as a continental nation, both in the land mass they occupy and in attitude. With the exception of the missile bases installed in Cuba in 1962, the direct challenges they have presented to date have been supported primarily by their land power.

The Soviet Army is a vast organization; its strength is in the neighborhood of 2.5 million men. It is a well-trained, well-armed, and well-led force. Its tactics are modern, and it has the mobility and the firepower to make it a formidable foe. It is the most heavily armored force in the world, estimated to possess some 55,000 tanks and armored artillery pieces—almost double the number in the U.S. Army. The Russians maintain about 150 line divisions in their standing establishment, of which between 80 and 100 may be considered combat-ready. To put this into proper perspective, it must be realized that a Soviet line division has a strength of 10,000–11,000 men, compared with approximately 15,000 in a typical U.S. division. In the Soviet scheme of things, the air and missile forces are a part of the army. About half of all Soviet aircraft are tactical planes for support of ground forces. The Soviet Navy is currently the second largest in the world. Its most powerful element is the submarine fleet.

The Army of the People's Republic of China is also massive, although not quite so large as the Soviet forces. Numbering over 2 million, it is organized into almost 150 divisions of from 10,000 to 17,000 men each. Almost all are infantry divisions, but a few armored and airborne divisions are said to exist. The Chinese Army has been reorganized and modernized in recent years. A weapons standardization program has resulted in simplification and increased efficiency in the logistical system. Further logistical improvement has been accomplished by the activation of additional service and support units. Expansion and modernization of the military school system has raised the caliber of the Chinese officers and NCO's. The Communist Chinese Air Force is organized primarily for tactical support of ground elements. The Chinese Navy is small, light, and possesses little threat.

The forces of the two giants of the Communist world—the Soviet Union and Red China—are backed by the armies of the satellite nations. How effective these backup forces might prove in a conflict is not only a matter of their military potential but also a question of the political complexion of the situation. The feud between Red China and the Soviet Union has revealed that the Communist bloc is not as monolithic as has been supposed. While it must still be assumed that an East-West conflict would find the Communist bloc united, unquestioned unity can no longer be taken for granted. For Moscow's European satellites, the Warsaw Pact—the Soviet counterpart to NATO—serves as the Kremlin's instrument for unified command and control. However, the East German uprising of 1953, the workers' rebellion in Posnan, Poland, in 1956, and the 1956 Hungarian revolt indicate that the reliability of the satellite armies is not entirely assured.

Of all the satellites, Albania is of the least consequence militarily; its armed forces of 25,000 can be written off as not meriting attention. Bulgaria has about ten 10,000-man divisions of moderate effectiveness. The Czechoslovakian Army, well-trained and well-equipped, is organized into about 15 divisions, includes armored elements, and is considered faithful to Moscow. The East German Army is a relatively modern force of 60,000, but it appears to be limited by the Russians (who maintain 22 divisions in East Germany) for the most part to internal policing. The Hungarian Army was purged following the 1956 revolt and is only now returning to its former strength of more than 100,000. The Polish Army is one of the best of the satellite forces. It is about 200,000 strong and is well organized and well trained. Rumania's armed force is about the same size as Poland's, but it is not as modern or as effective. Command of the Rumanian Army has been assumed by Soviet officers; although they have overhauled the organization they have apparently not sought to create a first-rate fighting force. Possibly, they have been influenced by Rumania's flirtation with Red China. Of the remaining members of the Communist bloc, the largest and the best conventional forces are maintained by North Korea and North Viet-Nam. Each is well trained, well equipped, and well organized. The North Korean Army is estimated to number more than 300,000. Both armies include a high proportion of combat-experienced troops. Regular units of the North Vietnamese Army of at least regimental size have been positively identified in operation in South Viet-Nam.

The third prong of the trident is the demonstrated capacity —and the demonstrated intent—of the Communist bloc to instigate and support unconventional warfare, which includes such techniques as subversion, insurgency, and guerrilla warfare. These tactics were used successfully by the Communists in Indochina and in Cuba. They were attempted in Greece, in Malaya, and in the Philippines. Although on some levels the conflict in Viet-Nam merges into conventional warfare, for the most part it is unconventional.

Unconventional warfare by its very nature is unpredictable, nonconforming, aberrant, and wanton. It is hit-and-run attack with no front, no rear, and no flanks. It depends on stealth, speed, infiltration, subterfuge, and trickery. Its tactics include all of the "dirty" devices in the book: arson, murder, sabotage, ambush. The Communists single out as special targets government functionaries, local officials, village headmen, schoolteachers, public health aides, and public works administrators, and through eliminating them seek to eliminate the processes by which the established government functions. Physical attack is supplemented by political, economic, and psychological pressure in a thorough campaign of terror. The aim is to create chaos and the collapse of government so that the "new order" can step into the vacuum. The Communists invariably seek to picture themselves as liberators forced to adopt harsh measures as the only means of lifting the yoke of repressive government from the necks of the people.

The Strategic Response

In response to the nature of the Communist threat, and conditioned by the military potential of the Communist bloc, a comprehensive American military strategy has been formulated to contain and defeat the challenge. It is, naturally, a part of a larger national strategy that combines and coordinates into a mutually supporting whole all the sources of the nation's strength. From the purely military aspect, strategy is based on a flexible structure designed to afford options that can be called into play to suit the specific contingency. Under constant review in the light of changing conditions at home and abroad to make sure that it conforms to current circumstances and possibilities, this military strategy provides, in essence, the following major elements: (1) a balanced offensive-defensive combination to deter or, failing that, to retaliate for a nuclear attack; (2) a balanced land-sea-air combination to engage the enemy in the extended phase of a general war or to prevent a lesser conflict from escalating into a general war; (3) a capability for adequate, swift, long-range air and sea lift; (4) a system of collective security alliances and pacts; and (5) a capability to cope effectively with unconventional, guerrilla, or insurgency operations.

The balanced offensive-defensive force strategy conceived to contain and neutralize the nuclear threat is predicated upon two fundamental principles: credibility and survivability. To deter nuclear attack, the first objective of the strategy, the offensive portion of the force must be credible to the enemy—he must realize that it is potent enough to inflict unacceptable losses on him, and he must be convinced that the United States has the will to unleash a retaliatory attack. But there is also another aspect to credibility, and that is survival. To be fully credible, enough of the nation's nuclear strike force must survive an initial attack sufficiently intact to retaliate against the enemy in strength that is unacceptable to him. The offensive strike capability is furnished by the missiles and manned bombers of the Strategic Air Command and by the Polaris missiles aboard the submarines of the Atlantic Command. There can be no question of the awesome destructive potential of this nuclear strike force. Literally, it is a hell of a force. Survivability is built into the strategy in several ways. One way is redundancy; there is enough "overkill" capacity so that even after an initial attack is absorbed, the surviving portions of the force will be sufficient to eliminate primary targets. Another major survival factor is provided by the dispersal of retaliatory forces around the country, around the world, and under the seas. The enemy cannot possibly count on eliminating or even seriously crippling the dispersed retaliatory nuclear strength of the United States. Finally, survivability is enhanced by round-the-clock operation of early warning networks and of active air-defense systems. The Army's role in the over-all nuclear strategy is concentrated in this last aspect of the offensive-defensive combination. That role is fulfilled by the Army Air Defense Command of the tri-Service North American Air Defense Command.

The second element of the military strategy—a balanced land-sea-air combination to engage the enemy in the extended phase of a general war or to prevent a lesser conflict from escalating into a general war—directly involves the Army in its traditional ground-combat role. Operating in coordination with the other services under the Unified Combatant Command format, the Army is deployed strategically overseas and in reserve in the United States and possesses the ability to engage the enemy with nuclear or conventional weapons. The seventeen active Army divisions, the supporting and service units, and the reserve establishment are all trained, organized, and equipped for this mission.

(Both of the foregoing elements are treated at length in Chapter IX.)

Since World War II, the Army has disposed a major portion of its strength abroad in recognition of the fact that the defense of the United States does not begin at its own shores. Refinement of this concept of forward deployment led to the creation of the U.S. Army Forces Strike Command as a flexible, deployable force to buttress existing dispositions abroad. Without adequate strategic lift, Army deployments in Europe, in the Pacific, in Latin America, and in Alaska would become separate, static enclaves unable to look beyond their own internal resources and denied ready access to each other and to the contiguous states of the United States. The alternatives would be to provide each enclave in advance with all of the manpower and matériel it might possibly need to cope with any contingency—an impossible achievement—or to withdraw to "Fortress America" and thereby assure victory for the Communist bloc. It is no exaggeration to say that strategic mobility is a key underpinning to the entire spectrum of Army operation.

The fourth element of the basic military strategy—and, in a political sense, the one on which it is based—is the formation of a system of collective security pacts and alliances. The validity of this concept is as self-evident as the rationale for adequate sea and air lift. Obviously, neither the United States nor any other single country possesses all the military strength that might be required to cope with every possible situation. Equally apparent is the fact that the military challenge of the Communist bloc is not directed against the United States alone. A system of alliances provides a framework for coordinating and pooling the Free World's military strength as a means of containing the common threat. In effect, it adds a new level of deterrence against Communist expansionism.

Of the security arrangements to which the United States is committed, four are multilateral alliances whose members have a basic community of interest in a specific geographical area. These alliances are: the North Atlantic Treaty Organization, or NATO; the Australia–New Zealand–United States Treaty, or ANZUS; the Southeast Asia Treaty Organization, or SEATO; and The Inter-American Treaty of Reciprocal Assistance, or the Rio Treaty. The United States also maintains a special relationship with a fifth alliance, the Central Treaty

Organization, or CENTO. Although not a member of CENTO, the United States cooperates closely in assisting the members (Iran, Pakistan, Turkey, and the United Kingdom) in strengthening the united defense posture in the Middle East. The United States participates in CENTO military exercises, and Americans serve on a number of important CENTO committees.

One of the earliest U.S. commitments to collective security is the Rio Treaty, to which a total of twenty American nations subscribe. The key provision of the Treaty is the principle that an attack against any American state is an attack against all and that each will come to the assistance of the others. The Rio Treaty is considered to embrace North and South America, Greenland, Antarctica, and the Arctic; it is not limited to armed attack from abroad but also extends, in Article 6, to all threats to the peace "other than armed attack." A chief contribution to the effectiveness of the Treaty as a peace-keeping instrument in the Americas is the United States undertaking, under the Rio Treaty, to assist in training the military forces of the signatories. Largely a responsibility of the U.S. Army, the training mission covers all phases of military operations. Training is conducted on site by Army teams assigned to the member countries, or in special courses at the U.S. Army School of the Americas at Fort Gulick, Canal Zone, or through enrollment of selected personnel in military schools operated in the continental United States.

As in the case of the Rio Treaty, the key to the North Atlantic Treaty Organization is the proviso that attack on one member is deemed an attack on all members. This clause gives NATO its strength as a deterrent, and it is undeniable that since NATO came into effect in 1949, Communist encroachment in Europe has been halted. NATO is a fifteen-nation alliance and enjoys a high degree of coordination and integration of the armed forces of thirteen of its members. Of the other two, Iceland cannot allocate troops in the common defense because the nation maintains no armed forces, and France has its own phenomenon—De Gaulle. Despite troubles with De Gaulle, NATO remains at this writing a powerful, viable alliance. Much of its visible strength, and hence much of its military deterrent power, stems from the presence of the U.S. Army in Europe and, especially, from USAREUR's Seventh Army, deployed along the Iron Curtain. In addition, the influence of the U.S. Army upon the military posture of the alliance is readily apparent throughout the NATO military structure in Europe.

The two remaining multilateral, mutual-security alliances to which the United States is committed—ANZUS and SEATO —are complementary in that they cover the Asian-Pacific area. SEATO includes the three members of ANZUS—Australia, New Zealand, and the United States—plus France, Pakistan, the Philippines, Thailand, and the United Kingdom. The SEATO charter recognizes that an attack upon one of the signatories represents a common threat to all but, unlike the NATO charter, it does not impose a treaty obligation to join in the common defense against the attack. The armed forces of SEATO nations participate in joint exercises but, again unlike NATO, they are not linked in a permanent, integrated military structure. As in SEATO, the ANZUS nations collaborate regularly in joint military training exercises. Both treaty organizations extend special emphasis to standardization among their military forces. Within SEATO, standardization is concentrated largely in the areas of tactics and operational doctrine; within ANZUS, the standardization program embraces weaponry and equipment.

In addition to its multilateral alliances, the United States is directly linked to some forty-five nations by bilateral, mutual assistance treaties and agreements. Four of the bilateral treaties are of special significance because of their scope or because of the sensitivity of the geography involved: the treaties with Japan, the Philippines, the Republic of China (Nationalist China), and the Republic of Korea (South Korea).

The agreement with Japan pledges both nations to resist an armed attack against either within Japanese territory and grants to the United States the use of military bases in Japan for certain, carefully defined purposes. The agreement with South Korea binds both nations to joint defense in the event either is attacked in Korea, and grants the United States broad rights to maintain bases and to deploy troops within Korea. Under terms of the treaty, the Korean Army has been almost completely re-equipped with U.S. Army weapons and material and has been trained in U.S. Army tactics and doctrine. The treaty with the Republic of China is a replica in all major respects of the mutal assistance agreement with the Republic of Korea— the primary difference being in the geographic area covered. The treaty with the Philippines binds the two nations in mutual aid in the event of attack on Philippine territory and permits the United States to maintain bases in the Philippines under specified conditions. There is a particular traditional harmony between the armed forces of the Philippines and of the United States, a consequence of the long history of intimate relationship between the two nations. This traditional intimacy is especially true of the ground forces. The Philippine Army is closely modeled after the U.S. Army, and its tactics and equipment are basically American. Under the terms of special Congressional legislation, four Filipinos at a time may be enrolled as cadets at West Point.

The fifth element of American military strategy in response to the Communist threat is one that, in many ways, is of particular and peculiar concern to the U.S. Army. The strategic requirement for a capability to combat subversion and guerrilla warfare falls largely on the Army. And it is natural that the Army should assume major responsibility for countering subversion and guerrilla operations, because the normal environment for unconventional warfare is the Army's domain— the land mass.

Today, the most active threat to peace, particularly in developing nations, is concentrated in the realm of unconventional warfare. This threat is expected to become even more acute. In view of its importance to Army planning and operations, the entire matter is considered in the following chapter.

VIII

Stability Operations

It is doubtful if ever in the history of warfare so much public attention has been concentrated so rapidly and fully on an aspect of conflict as that accorded to what is variously labeled stability operations, unconventional warfare, counterinsurgency operations, wars of national liberation, special operations, and guerrilla warfare. The profusion of terms is a reflection of the confusion that surrounds the subject. "Stability operations" seems as good an over-all designation as any. This term covers the application of the various elements of national power to restore peace and order within a country. Militarily, stability operations do not involve employment of nuclear weapons or overt attack by the regular forces of an aggressor nation. "Counterinsurgency" comprises the military, political, economic, psychological, and sociological actions taken to suppress the pressures, ranging from subversion to violent action, exerted by resistance groups in an effort to overthrow a duly constituted government. In today's context, insurgency falls short of civil war and is primarily fomented, supported, and exploited by the Communist bloc nations. "Guerrilla warfare" is the offensive military tactics employed by relatively small groups to reduce enemy combat effectiveness, industrial capacity, and morale. It is characterized by small-scale, violent actions of short duration. "Unconventional warfare" embraces guerrilla operations, evasion and escape, and subversion and is usually conducted in enemy or enemy-controlled territory by predominantly indigenous forces supported externally. "Wars of national liberation" is a term introduced by Nikita Khrushchev in 1961 to cover the increasingly popular Communist device of fostering and supporting insurgency and subversion within a country as a subterfuge to mask covert aggression against the stabilized government. "Special operations" used to mean simply military maneuvers requiring specialized troops, equipment, or techniques; within the context of the times the term has become synonymous with unconventional warfare.

The proliferation of terms—and the fine distinctions and quibbles over definitions—is unimportant. What is important is that in the past fifteen years this long-time Communist strategy has been more and more widely used. Nuclear threat remains suspended over the Free World, but nuclear attack by the enemy carries with it the assurance of devastating nuclear retaliation and so, at least to a degree, there is a certain mutual canceling-out of the nuclear arsenals. The threat of conventional attack remains valid and the Communist standing armies of 5 million or so men surely emphasize its validity; but here, too, there is an undeniable deterrence in the roughly equal size of the Free World's standing armies and in their willingness and ability, demonstrated in Korea, to meet overt aggression with force. Thus, Communist support of wars of national liberation as an increasingly active strategy attains major significance, the more so because of its eagerness to utilize and extend the techniques of twilight war.

Insurgency itself is no latter-day innovation. As early as 1787, the United States itself had a taste of insurgency when it became necessary to call out a militia force in Massachusetts to put down a rebellion led by Daniel Shays. In 1794, President Washington summoned 15,000 militiamen from four states to quell the Whiskey Rebellion in Pennsylvania. A century later, the United States was embroiled in counterinsurgency in the Philippines, then under American administration. For three frustrating years, a superior joint American-Filipino force pursued elusive guerrilla bands through the jungles before they succeeded in subduing the insurgents. All of these insurgencies were domestic issues, internally generated and internally supported and directed. Not until the years of both Fascist and Communist subversion between World War I and World War II was insurgency expanded into an international tool. And not until after World War II did it assume its present global shape.

The Military Assistance Program

In the post-World War II international scene, the United States emerged as the major power possessing both the resources to embark on a massive program of international reconstruction and the moral purpose to accept such responsibility. Moreover, and perhaps even more compellingly, enlightened self-interest made it mandatory that the United States undertake to bring order and progress to the war-torn nations, for it quickly became evident that the security of America depended in large measure on a community of stable, thriving nations. To put it another way, it was obvious that weak, disordered nations would be prime targets and feeble opponents for Communist expansionism. Without American assistance, there was every likelihood that many of these nations would fall victim to Moscow, and the Red tide would swirl closer to American shores. Whatever the fundamental motivations for American assumption of the role of international rebuilder—compassion, generosity, morality, or self-protection—it had become clear that "no foreign entanglement" as a predominating policy in the national life of the United States had joined the dodo.

In February, 1946, Secretary of State Byrnes declared that the United States neither would nor could "stand aloof if force or the threat of force is used contrary to the purposes and principles" of the U.N. Charter. In early 1947, President Truman enunciated the Truman Policy, which called for containment of Soviet imperialism, provided military and economic assistance to Greece and Turkey to strengthen their abilities to resist Communist pressures, and pledged the United States to supply aid anywhere in Europe where aggression threatened, whether by subversion or by overt attack. In the same year, General George C. Marshall, who had succeeded Secretary Byrnes, proposed an aid program that, for magnitude and generosity, was unprecedented in the annals of world history. The program became law in 1948 when Congress approved the Foreign Assistance Act, more popularly known as the Marshall Plan. A key feature was that the United States would provide the financing, but the participating nations would formulate their own reconstruction plans, not only to provide quick relief for their tortured economies but—and more important in the long view—"to permit the emergence of political and social conditions in which free institutions can flourish." (In the next dozen years some $80 billion in U.S. foreign aid was appropriated.) In 1949, the North Atlantic Treaty Organization came into being. Although NATO supports cooperation of its member nations in a number of fields, the heart of the treaty is military cooperation. The United States, as one of its contributions, negotiated a series of bilateral agreements with member nations whereby direct American military aid was furnished to bolster the armed strength of the NATO countries. In the first ten years of operation, the American military aid program for NATO nations amounted to some $20 billion.

All of these measures were effective in containing Soviet imperialism in Europe. A stabilized western Europe, its armies refurbished, refitted, mutually supporting, and backed by the resources of the United States, its territories protected by the American nuclear arsenal, no longer presented its earlier temptation to Soviet adventurers. Stalemated in one direction, the Communist bloc sought targets of opportunity in other directions. New targets were not hard to find.

Pent-up aspirations for national independence had for years been sleeping volcanoes in many areas of the world, particularly in Asia and Africa. In the post-World War II period, the volcanoes began to spew lava. From the smoke of their eruptions, an accelerating string of new nations commenced to appear. The changes introduced within these emerging nations were profound, revolutionary in the broadest sense of the term. By the inherent nature of revolutionary change, an atmosphere of turmoil and strain prevails, a condition conducive to violence. Aggravating everything was the long history of conflict and frustration within many of the new nations, and their lack of a tradition of democratic government and a firmly established national identity. All of these circumstances created situations tailor-made for Communist exploitation. The Communist threat, contained in Europe, shifted its focus to the other continents. To thwart this acute menace to peace, the United States extended to the new nations—and to the troubled nations of Latin America—its system of bilateral aid agreements because, unaided, they had little with which to present an adequate defense against subversion, coercion, and "wars of national liberation." Thus, the United States found itself engaged in fostering the internal development and assisting in the internal defense of scores of nations.

These stability operations are more than simply military programs. They are a comprehensive, coordinated, multifaceted approach designed for attack against the root causes of instability—economic, social, psychological, and political. Implicit in all of these efforts is a fundamental requirement for internal order and peace. The military phase of the assistance program cannot be underestimated because it creates the climate within which the other aspects of the over-all aid effort can flourish. However, the military phase must be placed in proper context; it is not an end in itself and it cannot be divorced from the entire program of which it is a part.

Major responsibility for the military assistance effort rests with the Army since the military threat facing the emerging nations is very largely, indeed almost exclusively, within the ground environment. Consequently, it is on the ground that it must be met and defeated. The problem confronting the Army in dealing with the emerging nations required a new approach.

It was not merely a matter of working with its European-style military assistance mission transferred to a new geographic setting. Nor was it simply a question of how to assist in the arming, equipping, and funding of a national military force, as had, for the most part, been the case in Europe. To a great extent, these were armies that were technically unsophisticated and naïve, inadequately trained, even in the fundamentals of military operations, poorly armed and organized, and often viewed with mistrust and suspicion by large segments of the indigenous population. The task of the U.S. Army was to create in these forces a new order of military capabilities, and, at the same time, to assist them in gaining the support and confidence of their own people. It was, and is, a task requiring a high degree of tact and understanding, thorough professionalism, and an assumption of numerous activities that are only peripherally military in character.

In recent years, Viet-Nam has provided the most dramatic example of the Communist use of subversion and insurgency as a device to mask aggression. The over-all U.S. assistance program to counter that insurgency has utilized a "team" approach controlled and directed by the United States Mission to Viet-Nam, headed by the U.S. ambassador. The agencies responsive to the ambassador, each of them charged with a segment of the over-all assistance program, are the U.S. Embassy (concerned primarily with political stabilization), the U.S. Operations Mission (involved with social and economic development), the U.S. Information Service (to deal with information and psychological operations), and the Military Assistance Command, Viet-Nam (MACV) (responsible for military security matters).

MACV is a tri-service agency that commands and controls the total American military commitment in South Viet-Nam. In its relationship to the U.S. combat units fighting there, MACV functions as any other joint U.S. headquarters directing active operations. In its relationship to the Vietnamese armed forces, MACV embodies the advisory functions normally assumed by a U.S. military advisory group. It is the latter role that is discussed in this chapter.

Approximately 90 per cent of the strength of Viet-Nam's regular forces is in the ground elements, and this preponderance is reflected by a corresponding weighting of U.S. military advisers in favor of the Army. U.S. Army field advisory detachments are assigned to Vietnamese Army units down to battalion level (and sometimes down to companies), to province and key district chiefs who are responsible for the employment of regular and paramilitary forces, and to the principal training centers and military schools. The advisers serve as planners, tacticians, trainers, logisticians, and counselors on the whole range of military science. They must necessarily possess a very high degree of professionalism. More than that, the advisers need to have a large measure of tact and a persuasive tongue, since they are dealing with a sovereign people who are sensitive and proud and are not compelled to heed the advice proffered.

In their training role, advisory personnel are dispersed to some 225 separate locations in the Republic of Viet-Nam where they assist in a major effort to upgrade the level of military instruction. Emphasis is accorded to leadership training, marksmanship, squad tactics, security, scouting and patrolling, ambush and defense against ambush, night operations, physical conditioning, intelligence collection, and civic actions. This last activity has become prominent in military operations, and it is a significant part of the total stabilization program. In essence, it is an attempt to win the confidence and support of the population by putting military abilities to use for the benefit of the local community. Army medical personnel, for example, assist villagers in improving their health practices and in establishing local health facilities, however rudimentary and limited they might be. Army engineers assist in laying out drainage ditches, serviceable bridging, and similar public works. Other military specialists devote their peculiar talents, wherever possible and appropriate, to projects that improve the social and economic conditions, especially in rural areas where the need is greatest. All of this is supplementary to the basic improvement programs conducted by the U.S. Operations Mission. The benefits of the civic actions are twofold: an improvement in the conditions under which the population lives and an improvement in civilian regard for the military.

In their role with the Vietnamese combat units in the field, U.S. advisers assist in planning tactical missions, and they accompany the units in the execution of tactical missions in order to observe the operation. This is a particularly delicate phase of the adviser's job because he exercises no command authority over the Vietnamese unit with which he is serving. How quickly and how fully his tactical advice is followed depends upon the kind of relationship he has succeeded in developing with the Vietnamese commander. It is a relationship that must, of necessity, be built on mutual respect, trust, and confidence. Advisory personnel accompanying combat missions as observers are not expected to be active participants in the action—or so goes the theory. In practice, U.S. advisers have the authority to call in U.S. tactical air strikes in support of an operation, and for that reason they cannot remain passive observers when a need for air support develops. An even more compelling reason for active participation is the fact that the Viet-Cong make every effort to single out advisory personnel as targets—a hazardous compliment to the merit of the advisory program.

Advisers assigned to district chiefs have a dual task. One responsibility is to assist in training the Popular and Regional Forces, which consist of farmers in the area who serve as part-time soldiers for localized operations. The training is confined to basics, in consonance with the militarily unsophisticated nature of the farmer-soldiers and with the restricted area of operations. The second responsibility of the advisers is to aid the local representative of the U.S. Operations Mission in placing his social and economic improvements into effect.

There is a long historic precedent for military assistance

programs and for the attachment of professional soldiers to foreign armies. More than 2,000 years ago, Philip of Macedon relied on skilled Theban drillmasters to help train his troops. Some eighteen centuries later, the United States depended on von Steuben and other foreign officers for help in creating an effective Continental Army. But in the past, professionals attached to foreign armies have either exercised command or have been restricted to a training and technical role. The mission of the U.S. adviser, particularly in Viet-Nam, falls into an in-between area. He is not actually a commander, although his influence on command is pervasive; nor is he solely a trainer. His is an immensely complex role in which he is the supplier of arms and equipment, the tutor, monitor, psychologist, patient taskmaster, diplomat, mover and shaker, and soldier.

Advisers do not constitute a special corps or branch of the Army. They are selected from among promising candidates throughout the Army at large and then go through an intensive program of preparation for their assignments. Their preparation includes concentrated courses in language and area familiarization, counterinsurgency and guerrilla operations, psychological warfare, and the missions and functions of the other U.S. agencies that join in the total stabilization effort. The instruction is subject to continuing refinement and innovation as the Army seeks new and better ways to conduct stability operations and incorporates into its evolving doctrine lessons learned in the field.

Special Forces

In the mid-1960's the American public embarked on a Special Forces "binge." "The Ballad of the Green Berets" was playing on every transistor radio, and facsimiles of the distinctive Special Forces headgear were selling well at $1.98 each in souvenir shops. Press accounts, semifictional novels, even a comic strip, heralded the exploits of the Special Forces. Unfortunately, public acclaim is not always synonymous with public understanding. Much that has been published about the

Special Forces is inaccurate, and much that might have been said has not been. Special Forces have been hailed as an elite force within the Army, and this much is so—they are an elite force. But they are not a military distillation of "Batman," as the popularizers might lead one to assume. They are tough, resourceful, daring, but they are neither superhuman nor reckless. The criteria for Special Forces personnel emphasize steadiness, reliability, calmness, intelligence, maturity (their average age runs around thirty), and mastery of exacting military skills.

Special Forces exist for one essential role—unconventional warfare. They are a behind-the-enemy-lines organization. Whether by air-drop, air-landing, or other means of infiltration, they are designed for deep penetration into enemy-controlled territory to foster, organize, train, and, if necessary, command guerrilla and resistance movements. The fact that Special Forces units have been intimately involved in the Viet-Nam conflict as military advisers does not diminish their primary mission. Actually, their advisory employment derives from their basic role, for it is obvious that many of the techniques and skills of the Special Forces are particularly relevant to the demands of counterinsurgency. In selected subsectors in South Viet-Nam, Special Forces advisory teams are working with various indigenous tribes in the more remote areas in an effort to inculcate in these ethnic groupings a willingness to resist the Viet-Cong and the basic military ability required to do so successfully.

As a separate entity within the Army, Special Forces is a recent concept, but as a technique of warfare, unconventional operations have frequently been adopted by the Army. Historic spiritual predecessors of the Special Forces include Francis Marion and his Revolutionary War "Swamp Foxes" and Brigadier General Frank D. Merrill and his World War II "Marauders."

When the Korean War stimulated the expansion of U.S. military resources, the Army reappraised its range of capabilities, and the fresh assessment led to the establishment of the Special Warfare Center at Fort Bragg, North Carolina. The logic on which this decision was based is that in the event of a third world war, there would be a need for trained units able to conduct guerrilla operations behind enemy lines as a rear-area extension of the "big war" at the front. The Special Warfare Center was to organize and train guerrilla units that would be used to harass the enemy deep in his own territory. The center began to face up to its task, but it received only half-hearted support because the then dominant strategy of the Joint Chiefs of Staff was the concept of massive retaliation. Unconventional warfare is the very antithesis of nuclear response, and the emphasis on big war left the Army little opportunity to prepare itself for anything else. With the Army's major effort directed toward building an arsenal of missiles, rockets, tanks, and big guns, Special Forces came out a poor second best. To President Kennedy belongs the most credit for rescuing the Special Warfare Center from the doldrums. Recognizing that unconventional warfare was perhaps the likeliest form of conflict within the context of the times, he directed that the center receive the necessary support for build-up of a positive capability for guerrilla and antiguerrilla operations. It was President Kennedy who authorized the wearing of the berets by Special Forces. Later, following the President's assassination, the center was fittingly renamed the John F. Kennedy Center for Special Warfare.

In 1952, the Army's first Special Forces unit was formally activated at the center. From that modest beginning has grown a corps of between 10,000 and 15,000 men organized into six Special Action Forces (SAFs). Five of the SAFs are regionally oriented; that is to say, each of the five is intensively trained in the language, customs, religions, cultures, history, politics, and geography of a specific region, in addition to being trained in all of the techniques of unconventional warfare. Thus, there are SAFs oriented toward Asia, Latin America, Europe, the Middle East, and Africa. The sixth SAF is a U.S.-based reserve available as a source of replacements for the others, as a source of cadres around which additional SAFs can be formed, or as a deployable force to meet emergency requirements abroad. Each SAF is tailored to the nature of its geographic area of responsibility and can be augmented as necessary by increments of medical, civil affairs, psychological warfare, engineering, or other technical units.

Within each SAF are a variable number of Special Forces groups, each consisting of two or more Special Forces companies of 50 officers and 200 enlisted men. The company is broken down into teams, the basic operational unit. An "A" team, the smallest formation, consists of two officers and ten men. This mere dozen is equal to the enormous task of creating an indigenous guerrilla force that might run as high as 1,000 men. A "B" team, consisting of six officers and seventeen enlisted men, is designed to supervise and support several "A" teams. Each Special Forces company also includes a single "C" team to coordinate the operations of the "A" and "B" teams dispersed over a wide area. Each team is designed either for sustained, independent operations or for functioning in a team-company-group complex.

The emphasis on extremely small units is dictated by the nature of guerrilla warfare, in which combat is characterized by stealth, surprise, aggressive patrolling, violent attack, and rapid dispersal. Because the units are so small, each member shares an unusually high burden of personal responsibility. Not only is he a fully competent guerrilla and counterguerrilla fighter, but he is also specialized in a technical field such as weaponry, basic medicine, communications, or demolitions. Beyond that, he has a secondary capability in two fields other than his primary specialization. He is not simply generally familiar with his field; he is expert. A medically trained enlisted man can amputate a limb, treat a gunshot wound, or deliver a baby. (During a tour with the Meo tribesmen of Laos, one medic delivered thirty-two babies.) The weapons expert can cope with virtually any foreign weapon, even obsolete models. The demolitions man can convert chemical fertilizer into explosives. All of this specialization is superimposed upon the fundamental training in unconventional tactics and upon a long, rigorous course of physical conditioning that includes hand-to-hand combat and survival techniques. Finally, the Special Forces soldier is a qualified paratrooper. Unquestionably, he is the most broadly and intensively trained of any soldier in any army.

IX

Joint Operations and the Combatant Commands

The Army has an interesting record of joint association with each of the other services. In 1789, the government placed the fledgling Navy under control of the War Department. Chafing with irritation in the shadow of the Army, the minuscule Navy organized a lobby to bring pressure on Congress for creation of a separate Navy Department. Gestation proved a long-term affair; a full nine years passed before Congress finally brought forth an independent Navy Department. The Marine Corps, in its early days, fretted in the shadow of both the Army and the Navy, being obliged to adhere to Army regulations on land and to Navy regulations at sea. Adopting an understandable "plague-on-both-your-houses" attitude, the Corps pumped for authority to issue its own regulations, an authority eventually granted. The Air Force, of course, drew first breath as an internal branch of the Army. (The "revolt" of the airmen, and their success in ultimately obtaining independent and coequal status with the Army, is dealt with in some detail in Chapter X.)

Even the most sanguine of observers would not have mistaken these joint associations as a sound springboard for launching joint operations as the term is understood today. They did not provide for integrated planning for a common objective and under common control; above all, they did not embrace a joint tactical response rooted in a mutually shared doctrine and engendered by a fixed belief in a common strategic concept.

Until the advent of World War II, such joint operations as existed had been initiated by individual agreement between the services to meet a specific tactical requirement, such as the Army-Navy amphibious landings during the Mexican War. It is true that the Joint Army-Navy Board was organized in 1903, but it was completely without authority, its purpose being merely to make recommendations to the Secretary of War and to the Secretary of the Navy on matters referred to it and involving Army-Navy cooperation. Except for temporary, short-term joint operations adopted by negotiations between the two, the Army and the Navy went their separate ways, planning and operating independently of each other, and making individual, uncoordinated presentations to Congress for money and manpower. Only at the ultimate level, through the President in his role as Commander in Chief, could the services be considered linked by unity of command, of objectives, and of strategic concepts. It was a tenuous link.

The Army saw war as land war. The Navy saw it as sea war. Later, when war grew wings, the airmen saw it as air war. The glasses the military peered through were fogged with parochialism; few could discern war clearly as joint conflict, to be approached jointly and to be prosecuted jointly, with each service contributing its peculiar prowess to an over-all design. Modern war is not divisible by environment—tactics and aspects of strategy, yes, but not war as a whole.

The tremendously accelerated tempo, the vastly enlarged arena, the flexibility and mobility that have become the hallmarks of modern conflict have made it a joint affair. The Navy has the capability for striking targets far inland, the Army has taken to the air; the Air Force is charged with tactical support of ground forces; soldiers protect ground installations of the Navy and the Air Force; the Navy and Air Force furnish the Army with strategic sea- and air-lift. The interplay and interdependence of the services make it inescapable that they operate jointly within a system for unified direction and control.

The painting by John Trumbull shows the surrender of British forces under Lord Charles Cornwallis to the Commander in Chief of the Continental Army, George Washington, at Yorktown, Virginia, in 1781.

In this drawing by H. Billings, U.S. troops commanded by General Winfield Scott storm the fortress of Chapultapec, Mexico City, in 1846.

The Army's first amphibious operation, the troop landing at Vera Cruz, in 1846, during the Mexican War, is seen in a Currier and Ives lithograph.

Matthew Brady, following the Union forces into battle at Fredericksburg, Virginia, in 1863, took the first photograph of the U.S. Army in combat.

"Teddy" Roosevelt and the "Rough Riders" during the Spanish-American War, 1898, at San Juan Hill, Puerto Rico.

A Signal Corps "right-of-way" party shown tenting out in Alaska, 1908.

Secretary of War Newton D. Baker draws a number in the World War I draft, the first large-scale U.S. conscription of troops.

U.S. soldiers set up a 37-mm. gun during the Meuse-Argonne offensive, World War I, in France.

Troops of the 37th Division, supported by light tanks, destroy remaining pockets of Japanese resistance on Bougainville, Solomon Islands, 1944.

D day, June 6, 1944: General Dwight D. Eisenhower briefs a group of paratroopers just before the invasion of France.

Soldiers of the 84th Division in snow-covered fields near Amonines, Belgium, January, 1945, support units crippled by the German counterthrust in the Battle of the Bulge.

Some recent developments that increase the Army's mobility are the Chaparral launch vehicle (above left), made up of an infrared heat-seeking surface-to-air missile mounted on a modified Army self-propelled tracked vehicle to protect forward-area units against low-altitude air attack; a 16-ton GOER cargo carrier (above right), a highly maneuverable truck that "swims," churns through 3-feet-deep mud, climbs obstacles, and maintains a highway speed of more than 30 m.p.h.; and a 14-ton aluminum alloy bridge (below), hydraulically operated, that rides a standard M60 tank chassis, moves along a road at 30 m.p.h., and "scissors" open to span a 60-foot gap without exposing the operator of the mechanism to the foe.

Helmet-mounted infrared binoculars that let a driver see in the dark without any lights on his vehicle are one of many new devices invented in U.S. Army programs for research and development.

Another new development of Army research is this tiny "manpackradio" that receives coded dots and dashes and converts them to letters, letting untrained soldiers get messages effectively when voice cannot be used.

The need for a unifying apparatus became immediately apparent in World War II. A war on a global scale requiring total commitment of all resources in sustained land, sea, and air combat could be prosecuted successfully only through an over-all, joint directing authority responsible to the President as Commander in Chief. To fill this need, the Joint Chiefs of Staff was created in early 1942. The JCS, comprising the senior uniformed chief of each of the services, constituted the U.S. representation to the Combined Chiefs of Staff, whose other members were the British equivalent of the JCS. The function of the Combined Chiefs was to plan Allied strategy and Allied military collaboration. The JCS functions were never formally defined during the war but, in essence, they fell into two broad areas. The first of these was advising the President on strategic concepts, on military manpower and matériel requirements, and on matters of joint Army-Navy policy. The second was formulating joint strategic plans, under the direction of the President, and issuing the implementing orders to put those plans into operation. These orders were issued to theater commanders appointed by the President to exercise command over all U.S. Armed Forces within their respective jurisdictions, regardless of the service component of the units involved. Thus, a wartime organization for the joint employment of forces was established. It functioned imperfectly, especially in the Pacific, but well enough to get the job done. The joint Army-Navy Board that had been created in 1903 and that was still in being was not wiped off the books; it was permitted to decline gracefully and eventually to expire. Few mourned its passing.

After the experience of World War II, there could be no question of the absolute necessity for an effective, permanent structure to plan and direct the joint effort of the nation's military forces. The need was only intensified by the introduction of nuclear weapons and other technological advances, and by the emergence of Communist strength as a clear military threat to the Free World. A response to this need was embodied in the National Security Act of 1947 and in its subsequent amendments. With the stroke of the pen that validated the act, greater change was wrought in the military pattern of the United States than had ensued in the entire previous life of the Republic. The Act created a National Security Council, a Department of Defense, a permanent Joint Chiefs of Staff, a Department of the Air Force, and certain lesser agencies. The significance of this legislation is overwhelming.

The National Security Council, the highest statutory body whose functions pertain exclusively to the military security of the country, is in no way a part of the national military establishment as such, but its influence upon the services is profound. The pre-eminent position of the Council is implicit in the character of its membership: the President, the Secretaries of State, Defense, Army, Navy, and Air Force, and the Chairman of the National Security Resources Board. The obligation of the Council is to advise the President on formulation and integration of military, foreign, and domestic policies bearing on national security. In addition, the National Security Council exercises general direction over the Central Intelligence Agency. From the advice submitted, the President determines and defines the national security objectives. These, in turn, shape and define the military objectives. Thus, the genesis of the national military strategy—indeed of the entire military effort—is found within the recommendations submitted by the National Security Council to the President.

In creating the Department of Defense, the National Security Act of 1947 rendered a profound service to the nation's need for coherence among the services. By introducing a single authority, inferior only to the President, and empowered to make armed forces–wide decisions consistent with the wishes of the President, a stumbling-block to unity of the services was removed. The failure of the joint Army-Navy Board to achieve concrete results had amply demonstrated the futility of expecting meaningful, timely joint military actions to emerge from a committee of partisan members who had no authority save to report to party headquarters. By the terms of the act, the Secretary of Defense became the over-all military decision-maker, under the authority of the President. There was now a single voice on interservice affairs where previously there had been a chorus frequently singing in different keys.

The Joint Chiefs of Staff, created in urgency upon the entrance of the United States into World War II and never disestablished at the termination of that war, was accorded legal status by the National Security Act of 1947. Membership of JCS consists of the Chairman, appointed by the President from each of the services in rotation (although the President is not bound to rotate the post), and the Chief of Staff, or the equivalent, of each of the services. When the Joint Chiefs consider matters pertaining to the Marines, the Commandant of the Marine Corps sits as a coequal of the regular members.

The broad JCS mission is to serve as principal military adviser to the President, to the National Security Council, and to the Secretary of Defense. The specific JCS responsibilities embrace preparation of strategic plans and direction of strategic employment of the military forces, preparation of joint logistic plans and assignment of responsibilities to the services in accordance with those plans, establishment of unified combatant commands in strategic areas, formulation of policies for joint training of the military forces, and the review of major manpower and matériel requirements of the military forces in accordance with strategic and logistic plans.

It is important to recognize what the Joint Chiefs are and what they are not. They are responsible for the strategic direction of the military forces. This removes from the military departments any command authority over their combatant forces, but leaves them the functions of recruiting, mobilizing, training, organizing, equipping, and administering their troops, and furnishing forces to the unified combatant commands established by the Joint Chiefs. However, this does not mean that the command authority lost by the military departments has been gained by the Joint Chiefs. Congress, in a statement of policy embodied in the National Security Act of 1947, was quite clear on this point, specifically prohibiting the Joint

Chiefs from constituting themselves a single Chief of Staff over the services. All orders issued to the combatant commands by the JCS are transmitted in the name of the Secretary of Defense and by his authority, as approved by the President.

As a consequence of the statutory establishment of the Joint Chiefs, there are now two command channels from the President–Secretary of Defense level to the military forces. Via one channel, operational orders are issued through JCS to the combatant commanders, bypassing the military departments. Via the second channel, orders on all other matters are issued to the military departments. Little noted by the public, and not fully appreciated even by some of the men in uniform, is the existence of the first chain of command, a channel that removes from the military departments any operational authority over their own combat forces. The purpose is to preclude any partisan dilution or interpretation by the military departments of the strategy conceived by the Joint Chiefs and approved by the Secretary of Defense.

That is not to say that doctrinaire concepts of the military departments are unheeded. The Joint Chiefs, after all, are composed of the Chief of Staff of each of the services. Appointment to JCS can hardly eradicate beliefs formed in a professional lifetime nourished by service doctrine. Thus, in their efforts to arrive at joint solutions to their problems, the Joint Chiefs have the benefit of authoritative exposure to the views of all the services. Where JCS cannot reach agreement on an issue, the divergent views, and the justification for each, are presented to the Secretary of Defense for decision.

Some critics of the JCS system disdain the apparent incongruity of a corporate chiefs of staff and the impracticability of a "military collective" to plan and direct the nation's military strategy. There are two arguments to buttress the case for the Joint Chiefs. First, battlefield command is not pluralistic; it is exercised by a single, responsible commander and it should not be confused with the off-the-battlefield deliberations of JCS. Second, the Joint Chiefs have been in business since 1942, and, during all of the ensuing years, although the balance sheet may have had its lean years, bankruptcy of the national military establishment has never been a threat.

The Joint Chiefs are only four in number—or five, counting the Commandant of the Marine Corps—and it is obvious that they must have a staff to assist them in the discharge of their world-wide, services-wide responsibilities. It was for this purpose that the National Security Act of 1947 created the Joint Staff. Initially limited to a strength of 100 officers, the Joint Staff was progressively expanded by legislative amendment to 210 and then to 400. This numerical limitation is exceeded today, with the knowledge and tacit approval of Congress, by establishment in the Pentagon of a vague entity known as the Organization of the JCS. In all, the total staff assisting the Joint Chiefs runs close to 2,000.

The Joint Staff proper is divided into directorates to cope with most of the usual affairs of a normal military staff—personnel, operations, logistics, plans and policy, and communications-electronics. To these functional areas is added another staff division: Special Assistant for Counterinsurgency and Special Activities. Within the amorphous organization of the JCS are a number of committees and agencies devoted to such matters as military assistance, liaison with NATO, arms control, joint war games, joint command and control, nuclear affairs, strategic mobility, and meteorology.

Congress clearly spelled out its intent that the "joint staff shall not operate or be organized as an over-all armed forces general staff and shall have no executive authority." Just as clear is the inescapable fact that the staff that serves the Joint Chiefs has many of the attributes of an armed forces general staff. This is an inevitable development, despite legislative prohibition, because the complexity of modern war requires a unified response. Such a requirement is not satisfied by merely providing unified combatant commands; their effectiveness is seriously diminished if there is a failure to provide a mechanism for joint staff support of the joint field operations.

The Congressional ban on an armed forces general staff is predicated on a fear of "Prussianization" of the top military hierarchy, a fear of a made-in-America version of the self-perpetuating Imperial German General Staff. This ignores the fact that even if such a development were philosophically possible, it is legally impossible. The legislation that established the Joint Staff specifically limits the tenure of members to three years and bans reassignment to the staff for a minimum of three succeeding years; it permits a maximum of thirty exceptions to the three-year waiting period, and then only with the express approval of the Secretary of Defense. Thus, self-perpetuation is effectively precluded. It seems reasonable to assume that Congress recognizes both the adequacy of the legislative safeguards and the validity of the military requirements for some form of joint general staff, and for those reasons chooses to permit both the creation of the organization of the JCS and the assumption of many general staff attributes.

The National Security Act of 1947, which wrought such massive and sweeping change in the military structure of the United States, introduced a curious paradox when it disengaged the Air Force from the possessive embrace of the Army and made it a separate, independent service administered by its own military department. In a very real sense, the tactical ground and the tactical air elements must be a battlefield team with unity of control, integration of planning, and coordination of execution. Such an integrated response by the battlefield ground and air elements became much more difficult to achieve after the Air Force became independent of the Army. This is not to imply that there were not sound reasons for the "unification" action, as it was called with semantic inconsistency. But these reasons lay outside the unquestionable need for integrity of the ground-air team. The saving grace was that within the Joint Chiefs and the Joint Staff was the means of achieving unity on the battlefield through the combatant commands that the Joint Chiefs were empowered to establish.

The instrument through which the military forces are jointly employed is the combatant command. Established by the Joint Chiefs of Staff in accordance with the strategic plans framed by them and approved by the Secretary of Defense, combatant commands are of two types: unified or specified. A unified combatant command is composed of units from two or more of the services and is responsible for "fighting" those units within a given geographic area. The unified commander exercises authority over all of his assigned units, regardless of the identity of the parent services concerned, and the staff of his headquarters is integrated through manning from the services from which his assigned units come.

The fundamental differences between unified and specified commands are that the mission of the specified command is functional rather than geographic, and that its forces are either entirely or preponderantly from a single service. Its role is to support the grand strategy by discharging the functional mission with which it is charged.

The Specified Combatant Commands

STRATEGIC AIR COMMAND

At present, there is only one specified combatant command in existence: the Strategic Air Command of the Air Force. The SAC function, under the direction of the Joint Chiefs, embraces strategic bombing on a world-wide basis. To do the job, SAC has a long-range air arsenal that includes all of the nation's strategic nuclear delivery capability, whether by missile or by bomber, except for the Polaris submarine fleet of the Navy.

SAC's gigantic command post, with three of its block-long floors underground, is the nerve center at Offut Air Force Base, Nebraska, from which the attack order would be flashed to strategic missile and bomber commanders. But the order would not originate with the SAC commander, for only the President is empowered to order a nuclear attack. The order would start with the President and be relayed to SAC instantaneously through the Joint Chiefs of Staff. On his own volition, the SAC commander can, and frequently does, order an alert to test the reflexes of the various elements of his command, located at some eighty sites in the United States and around the world.

The Unified Combatant Commands

There are seven unified combatant commands: the Alaskan Command, the Atlantic Command, the Continental Air Defense Command, the U.S. European Command, the Pacific Command, the Southern Command, and the United States Strike Command. In several respects, the newest of the unified commands, the U.S. Strike Command (USSTRICOM) is the most interesting of all. For that reason, it merits close inspection.

UNITED STATES STRIKE COMMAND

Much of the impetus for creation of USSTRICOM, established by the Joint Chiefs in 1961, stemmed from lessons learned in the 1958 crisis in Lebanon when the pro-Western Lebanese Government, threatened by revolt, appealed urgently for an American pacification force. Responding to the plea, the United States quickly dispatched an all-service task force and, just as promptly, recalled it when the crisis had passed. The operation accomplished its purpose, but in doing so it revealed certain major weaknesses of the American task force. First, the task force was hastily assembled by stripping units from the already existing unified commands, the only convenient source of available troops in a combat-ready posture. This expedient satisfied the need for speed in the deployment, but it left the losing commands in a weakened position, which in turn, raised the question of the ability of the understrength commands to fulfill their missions if an emergency presented itself before their lost units rejoined them. The second defect uncovered was the lack of a comprehensive, decisive, and instantly reactive system of command and control. Each service component of the task force had its own channel of communications to its own headquarters, and it depended upon this channel for the receipt of instructions. As a result, coordination became a cumbersome, long-distance affair. It was to preclude repetition of these deficiencies in future crises that USSTRICOM was established by the Joint Chiefs.

The fundamental purpose of USSTRICOM is to furnish rapidly deployable, combat-ready forces in an emergency situation calling for a response on a scale less than all-out nuclear war. It is meant to provide, within a conventional context, a tactical reaction as a balance to SAC's strategic, nuclear capability. The hope, of course, is that by the rapid movement of a conventional force to the scene of a crisis, the situation can be stabilized before it can escalate to a wider conflict. The operational plans for USSTRICOM present two alternatives, the choice to be determined by the location of the emergency. The first alternative provides for USSTRICOM combat elements to reinforce other unified commands and to serve under the authority of the receiving unified commander. The second alternative provides for USSTRICOM to operate independently in the Middle East, southern Asia, or Africa south of the Sahara. A two-service command (Army and Air Force), USSTRICOM is headquartered at MacDill Air Force Base, Florida, and is commanded by an Army general. The forces available to USSTRICOM include the combat-ready Army divisions and the Air Force tactical air wings in reserve in the continental United States.

USSTRICOM is organized into two major components: U.S. Army Forces Strike Command (ARSTRIKE) and U.S. Air Force Strike Command (AFSTRIKE). Both are headquartered in close proximity: ARSTRIKE at Fort Monroe, Virginia, and AFSTRIKE at adjacent Langley Air Force Base. It is not mere coincidence that Fort Monroe is also the home of the Continental Army Command—the CONARC commander does double duty as the ARSTRIKE commander. Furthermore, the forces earmarked for ARSTRIKE are drawn from the total CONARC resources. When not actually deployed with ARSTRIKE, either for training or for operations, the earmarked forces remain an integral part of CONARC's strategic reserve.

ARSTRIKE's strength is built around two corps: III Corps and XVIII Airborne Corps. Between them, the two corps normally consist of eight divisions that are in a state of readiness for ground combat. At any given time, a portion of this very potent striking force is prepared for deployment overseas within twenty-four hours. At all times, elements of the airborne units are on alert and are ready to board planes within one hour. The tactical air units that make up AFSTRIKE are prepared for the same high degree of reaction.

USSTRICOM's day-in, day-out emphasis is on building the capabilities already inherent in the ARSTRIKE and AFSTRIKE forces, on training them intensively and in depth for joint operations, on welding them into a smoothly functioning ground-air team, and on developing a recommended joint operational doctrine that is both compatible with the tactical characteristics of each of the services and consistent with the effective execution of USSTRICOM's mission. USSTRICOM's persistent and insistent emphasis on joint training, its unity of command, its single channel direct to the Joint Chiefs, its fully integrated staff, and its forces immediately available without stripping other unified commands, have effectively corrected all the deficiencies revealed by the Lebanon experience. A more subtle but highly significant factor is that the recommended ground-air operational doctrine evolved in USSTRICOM and the intimate relationship between ARSTRIKE and AFSTRIKE are rubbing off on both services. The ground-air relationship, so strained for some forty years and yet so vital to the military posture of the United States, is growing perceptibly better. (The ground-air relationship as a whole is examined in Chapter X.)

But USSTRICOM, potent and thriving, is only one of seven unified combatant commands. Each has its separate strategic responsibilities that collectively constitute a comprehensive grand design.

THE ALASKAN COMMAND

The Alaskan Command (ALCOM) is responsible for the defense of Alaska, including the Aleutian Islands and the islands of the Bering Sea but omitting air defense and the defense of sea communications. (The omitted portions of the defense responsibility are allocated to other unified combatant commands and will be covered a little further along.) Tri-service in composition, ALCOM is commanded by an Air Force general whose headquarters is at Elmendorf Air Force Base, near Anchorage. Nearby, at Fort Richardson, is the headquarters of ALCOM's ground element, U.S. Army Alaska (USARAL).

USARAL's mission is no sinecure—ground defense of almost 600,000 square miles of rugged country cut by fjords and mountains and booby-trapped with tundra, glaciers, and thick forests. These conditions are aggravated in much of Alaska by intense cold, pea-soup fog, and violent winds. To complete what is a difficult picture, roads are few, and, at its closest point, Alaska is separated from the Soviet Union's island territory by a strait little more than 2 miles wide.

A major problem for USARAL is the attainment of mobility and maneuverability in terrain that resists trespassers. To overcome terrain obstacles, USARAL depends on airlift and a large fleet of winterized vehicles with various ingenious systems of traction that provide a surprisingly good degree of cross-country mobility. The mechanical aids are supplemented by skis, snowshoes, and remote patrols by Eskimo Scouts of the Army National Guard. To condition soldiers for operations in snow country, USARAL operates the U.S. Army Northern Warfare Training Center at Fort Greeley.

USARAL's units are concentrated in the Anchorage-Fairbanks complexes. They consist primarily of infantry reinforced and supported by armor and Nike-Hercules anti-aircraft missile batteries. However, the ability of USARAL to perform its mission on a sustained or intensive basis in an emergency situation is limited without augmentation of its units. USARAL's troops from all units total the equivalent of little more than one division. When one considers that Alaska has an area of 586,400 square miles—an area equal to two Texases with enough left over for Alabama—that is indeed spreading the troops thin.

THE ATLANTIC COMMAND

The Atlantic Command (LANTCOM) is responsible for the defense of the Atlantic Ocean area and the western Indian Ocean, the Arabian Sea, and the western Bay of Bengal. With this vast expanse of water to guard, LANTCOM is obviously a Navy-oriented organization and is commanded by an admiral. The primary striking force is a powerful fleet built around an attack carrier force and missile cruisers and destroyers, supplemented by submarines possessing both a conventional and a nuclear capability and by aircraft operating from shore bases and from aircraft carriers. In support of this primary striking force is an amphibious assault element comprising transports, landing craft, assault helicopters, and command ships. The Army's role in the Atlantic Command is to provide ground forces for the amphibious assault element and for sustained combat ashore in the post-amphibious assault phase.

The Army component of the Atlantic Command is United States Army Atlantic (ARLANT). ARLANT came into being very hastily in 1962 as the Army component of the tri-service task force assembled in response to the Cuban missile crisis. When the Russians backed down in the face of the firm American stand, ARLANT troops were returned to their home stations and to their normal assignments, but ARLANT itself remained in being as a command structure. Thus, ARLANT is normally a head with no body. That is to say, ARLANT possesses no assigned troop units except in time of emergency, when it is fleshed out with ground units assigned from CONARC's strategic reserve. This permits tailoring the character and the composition of the ARLANT units to the pattern of the crisis and to the nature of the enemy. ARLANT maintains a permanent operating headquarters and a full staff on duty with the Atlantic Command at Norfolk, Virginia. It is the existence of the functioning ARLANT command structure that makes possible rapid assembly and deployment of the ground forces in accordance with ARLANT's contingency planning.

THE CONTINENTAL AIR DEFENSE COMMAND

Among the unified combatant commands, the position of the Continental Air Defense Command (CONAD) is unusual —it is the only unified combatant command that is itself a component of a larger unified command. CONAD is the U.S. element of the North American Air Defense Command (NORAD), an integrated, binational organization that includes United States and Canadian forces. The NORAD mission is to defend the North American continent from attack by air—an enormously complex task because attack can come at supersonic speed from virtually any direction on the compass. It can be spearheaded by manned bomber, by ground-launched intercontinental ballistic missile, by sea- or undersea-launched ballistic missile, by weapons launched from space vehicles. Thus, the air defenses must be flexible enough to match the weapons response to the nature of the attack, and must be sufficiently reactive to make all of the necessary decisions and determinations and issue the appropriate commands in mere minutes.

The tremendous problems involved in defending air attack divide themselves into four primary areas: detection, identification, interception, and destruction. Detection is performed by an extremely extensive, early-warning system comprising highly sophisticated radar "fences" that are extended offshore by airborne radar systems aboard long-range patrol planes. Identification, always tricky, is accomplished by two primary means: checking flight plans that advise of aircraft entering special zones (air defense identification zones) in which aircraft must identify themselves by radio as they enter, and visual inspecting by all-weather interceptor aircraft. Interception and destruction are closely related; interception is the electronic or other navigation of an air defense weapon, manned or unmanned, to its target so that it can identify and, if necessary, destroy the intruder.

NORAD is the dominant coordinator and controller of all North American resources for detection, identification, interception, and destruction of continental air-space intruders. It would, in event of an attack upon the continent, direct the battle for air defense. Within that context, CONAD's responsibility is to command and coordinate the U.S. components of the joint defense force when they are fulfilling purely national air defense missions. The NORAD/CONAD headquarters is located in Colorado Springs, Colorado, and is commanded by a U.S. Air Force general. The Army component of NORAD/ CONAD is the U.S. Army Air Defense Command (ARADCOM). ARADCOM's mission is to provide Army air defense forces for specified strategic areas that include most of the nation's major metropolitan centers, industrial complexes, and critical installations.

From its headquarters at Ent Air Force Base, Colorado, ARADCOM commands a continent-spanning web of surface-to-air missile emplacements that are manned and ready around the clock. All of the Army missile sites are an integral part of a system of NORAD/CONAD divisions and regions that are linked to each other and to the NORAD Combat Operations Center by dependable means of communications. Thus, all ARADCOM sites can be alerted instantly and simultaneously in the event of an emergency.

At present, ARADCOM depends upon two separate but complementary missiles: Nike-Hercules and Hawk. Both are supersonic, guided systems. Hawk is effective against low-flying aircraft at a sufficient lateral distance to afford an adequate margin of protection. Hercules, with a 75-mile range, is effective against high-flying aircraft at the limit of their attainable altitude. Maneuverable in flight to duplicate enemy evasive maneuvers, and with its nuclear warhead providing an extensive "kill" circle, a single Hercules can down a flight of enemy aircraft. ARADCOM maintains Hawk and Hercules in fixed sites, but Hawk, only 16 feet long, can be made mobile. The two weapons systems are subjected to a continuing process of improvement of their components. This process has repetitively upgraded their ability to acquire and track targets, to discriminate among targets, and to achieve accuracy.

Even more significant than ARADCOM's insistent enhancement of the weapons it possesses is its effort to perfect new systems. The current Nike-X program is a masterpiece of forward-looking development. From the Nike-X program has emerged the multifunction array radar, already successfully tested in prototype, to perform accurately and at lightning speed the acquisition, discrimination, tracking, and guidance functions that formerly required several separate radars. Two new missiles have been developed under the umbrella of Nike-X: Zeus and Sprint. Nuclear-tipped and capable of instantaneous, in-flight course changes, each is intended for interception and destruction of intercontinental ballistic missiles or submarine-launched ballistic missiles, and each has performed remarkably well in test firings. Zeus is designed for long-range intercepts, beyond the earth's atmosphere, and could be employed against hostile satellites. Sprint has an extraordinarily high rate of acceleration and is designed for short-range intercept of any missile that succeeds in penetrating the Zeus defenses. ARADCOM is also looking ahead to the SAM-D, a highly flexible missile system now in the terminal stages of development. SAM-D offers the possibility of employment against both enemy aircraft and short-range missiles, thus permitting a single system to do what now requires separate systems. Integration of these weapons systems into the operational air defense arsenal of ARADCOM hinges on the Department of Defense strategic and budgeting decisions. In the meantime,

ARADCOM remains in a state of constant readiness with the weapons it has on site, and it participates with the other service components of NORAD/CONAD in joint air defense exercises.

THE U.S. EUROPEAN COMMAND

The tri-service U.S. European Command (USEUCOM) is closely coordinated with the Allied forces that form the military resources of the North Atlantic Treaty Organization. USEUCOM, in fact, constitutes the bulwark of NATO's ready forces; its geographic sector of responsibility includes the European land areas of the members of NATO, and it is commanded by the same U.S. Army general who serves as NATO's supreme military commander in Europe.

The Army component of USEUCOM is United States Army Europe (USAREUR) with headquarters in Heidelberg, Germany. A potent organization, it comprises roughly 20 per cent of the entire manpower of the U.S. Army. The major striking force of USAREUR is the Seventh Army, concentrated in Germany along a front that faces the Iron Curtain. The forward element consists of a screening force of armored cavalry regiments patrolling the border regions shared with East Germany and Czechoslovakia. The Seventh Army has the strength to make it a credible deterrent to would-be aggressors. Its. divisions are well trained, highly maneuverable, versatile, and are supported by a comprehensive logistics system. It includes a heavy contingent of armor that is well suited to the character of the terrain in much of the area. Its weaponry is capable of conventional or nuclear response, and includes such persuasive hardware as Sergeant and Pershing missiles, Honest John rockets, self-propelled 155-mm. howitzers, self-propelled 175-mm. guns, and a wide array of armor. It will be even more persuasive when Lance, now well into the final developmental stage, replaces Honest John—thus substituting a weapon of greater range, finer accuracy, and improved cross-country mobility.

Much smaller than the Seventh Army, but possessing exceptional firepower for its size, is a second combat element of USAREUR: the Southern European Task Force (SETAF). Based on the plains of northeastern Italy, SETAF is a tactical nuclear missile force. Highly mobile in character, SETAF pursues a continuous cycle of training in order to maintain combat-readiness.

Smaller still than the 10,000-man SETAF is the Berlin Brigade. Normally built around three maneuver battalions, a reinforced tank company, and supporting units, the Berlin Brigade is not intended for sustained combat. It exists for two purposes. One is to be available to the German civil authorities to assist in riot control in West Berlin, should the need arise. The second purpose of the Berlin Brigade is to serve as trip-wire to discourage adventurism from the East.

USAREUR is a readily expandable force. It maintains in constantly usable condition sufficient weapons and equipment to fit out a maximum of two additional divisions that could be airlifted from the United States in an emergency. Unfortunately, France's 1966 withdrawal from its previous military cooperation within the framework of NATO is forcing USAREUR into a less advantageous position, causing reappraisal of strategic and tactical plans, reshuffling of the logistical network, and adoption of alternatives that are something less than ideal. In addition, some 40,000 highly trained troops were withdrawn from USAREUR units in 1966 to meet manpower needs created elsewhere by the pressures of the war in Viet-Nam; this personnel pinch will continue to be troublesome until the forces are fully replaced.

THE PACIFIC COMMAND

Unlike USEUCOM, which is largely a land mass with water on three flanks, the Pacific Command (PACOM) is a vast expanse of water containing a number of dispersed land areas. Both in manpower and in physical dimensions (some 85 million square miles), PACOM is the largest of the unified combatant commands. The jurisdiction of PACOM includes the Pacific Ocean and its islands (excepting the Aleutians), the Bering Sea (less its islands), the eastern Indian Ocean, Japan, Korea, and the countries of Southeast Asia. Since one of the Southeast Asian countries happens to be Viet-Nam, PACOM is, in a terribly literal sense, a combatant command. It is commanded by an admiral and is headquartered in Hawaii.

The Army component of PACOM is U.S. Army Pacific (USARPAC), which has its headquarters at Fort Shafter, Hawaii. USARPAC troop units are deployed along a 6,000-mile front distinguished by several regions of political and military turbulence. Geography bedevils USARPAC. Because of the great distances separating its deployed forces from one another and from Hawaii, and because of the extensive water barriers, USARPAC's logistical system depends on sea transport and airlift by the other services to a much greater extent than does any other overseas Army command. These same geographical factors create a necessity for organizational decentralization, resulting in segmentation of USARPAC's troop resources into five discontinuous areas: Hawaii, Japan, Korea, Okinawa, and Viet-Nam–Thailand.

The major ground unit in South Korea is the U.S. Eighth Army, emplaced in tactically tenable, defensive positions paralleling the demilitarized zone that bisects the peninsula. The positions are anchored on dominating terrain features and are laid out in sufficient depth to be an effective bar to rapid penetration from the north; they are dispersed enough to preclude easy immobilization by enemy air or nuclear attack.

The Eighth Army is a U.S. force in name but hardly in fact. Of its twenty divisions, only two are American; the remaining eighteen divisions are Korean, assigned to operational control of the Eighth Army and supplemented by token contributions from the Thai and Turkish armies. Even the two U.S. divisions are not wholly American; they depend on KATUSA (Korean Augmentation to the U.S. Army) to flesh out their ranks with Korean soldiers, making them the only American divisions that integrate foreign troops directly into their ranks. Fortunately, Eighth Army troops, whatever their nationality, are well trained and well equipped. They are backed by a comprehensive logistical network controlled by the 7th Logistical Command, but supply is complicated by the long haul via sea or air routes to keep stocks in Korea at the necessary levels. Despite all the complications of the situation, the Eighth Army is an energetic, combat-ready force.

The circumstances in Japan are radically different from those in Korea. USARPAC units in Japan are solely logistical in character. U.S. Army, Japan, maintains a logistical complex at Camp Zama that is capable of supporting a respectable combat element, but there are no U.S. ground combat units stationed in the country. Under the terms of the bilateral treaty by which Japan granted the United States the right to retain bases within her borders, it was mutually agreed that no use of the bases, save in the common defense within Japan, and no major changes in the character or composition of the U.S. forces or of their equipment would be undertaken without prior consultation with the Japanese authorities. This prohibition effectively rules out consideration of U.S. bases within Japan for support, either with matériel or with troop units, of the U.S. Army elements in other areas such as Viet-Nam, Okinawa, or Korea.

On Okinawa, USARPAC maintains both tactical and logistical troops. The tactical ground units on Okinawa are modest but fairly well balanced. They consist of IX Corps, an air defense brigade, and a rocket battalion. The logistical units retain their stocks in all categories at levels that are considerably in excess of their needs, maintaining surpluses that could be utilized in an emergency situation to fit out tactical units airlifted into the island.

Control of its far-flung units is exercised by USARPAC from its base in Hawaii. Normally, USARPAC also retains in Hawaii a readily deployable strategic reserve. Currently, the reserve has been severely reduced by allocation of units, including the 25th Infantry Division, from Hawaii to Viet-Nam. That is where the action is, and it follows that that is where the preponderance of PACOM's ground strength is to be found.

Of all the services, the Army represents the largest contingent in Viet-Nam. Its units are administered by a single, over-all headquarters: U.S. Army, Viet-Nam, which provides a direct channel from USARPAC to the ground element, but is not utilized for tactical direction of the force. Organizationally, U.S. Army, Viet-Nam, is a component of the U.S. Military Assistance Command, Viet-Nam (MACV). MACV is a unified command functioning under PACOM that exercises operational control and command over all U.S. military forces in Viet-Nam. An Army general, General W. C. Westmoreland, is the commander of both MACV and U.S. Army, Viet-Nam; it makes no difference which hat General Westmoreland happens to be wearing when he issues his orders to the Army component.

U.S. Army operations in Viet-Nam follow several avenues to the ultimate goal of securing the country against Communist aggression. Usually, the Army fights in reinforced company or battalion strength and, less frequently, in formations as large as a brigade. The war is really a continuing string of vicious little wars against a wily enemy who fights in small units that melt away and then reappear elsewhere without predictable pattern. No front or rear or flanks define the battlefield, and there is no sustained combat. In addition to its unilateral combat, the Army furnishes advisory teams to each Vietnamese Army corps, division, regiment, and battalion. At corps level, the U.S. Army teams assist in over-all planning and operations, and in such specialties as aviation, the use of paramilitary forces, medical services, logistics, communications, transport, artillery, ordnance, engineer, and civic actions. At levels below corps, the U.S. Army advisers accompany the Vietnamese units on combat missions. In addition, U.S. Army combat support units assist in Vietnamese combat operations by providing needed services such as helicopter ferrying of troops and supplies. And, as already described in Chapter VIII, a significant U.S. Army effort is conducted by Special Forces detachments that operate primarily in the more rugged and remote areas of the country, usually in sectors subject to strong Viet-Cong influence and control. Many of these regions are inhabited by primitive mountain tribes, and it is the task of the Special Forces detachments to teach the tribes the military fundamentals and to supervise their defense against Communist attack.

In Thailand, USARPAC maintains a considerable force of Army officers and men organized into the Military Assistance Advisory Group (MAAG) and a support element. The MAAG is responsible for assisting the Royal Thai Army in training, tactics, and the use and maintenance of weapons and matériel. MAAG personnel are assigned to all major Thai troop headquarters and units as instructors. The U.S. Army support element in Thailand includes engineer, signal, medical, aviation, ordnance, quartermaster, military police, transportation, and intelligence units, all of which are administered by the 9th Logistical Command.

THE SOUTHERN COMMAND

The United States Southern Command (SOUTHCOM) has an area of responsibility that embraces Central America (except Mexico) and South America. SOUTHCOM is a tri-service command headquartered in the Canal Zone. It is commanded by an Army general.

The Army component of SOUTHCOM is U.S. Army Forces, Southern Command (USARSO), based at Fort Amador, Canal Zone. The major, continuing mission of USARSO is the land defense of the Canal Zone. The total Army strength in the SOUTHCOM area is less than the equivalent of one division. USARSO tactical units consist of one brigade with an infantry, a mechanized, and an airborne battalion, a composite air defense missile battalion, and combat support units.

An unusual USARSO activity is the operation of the U.S.

Army School of the Americas at Fort Gulick, Canal Zone. The school curriculum runs the gamut of ground specialties, among them infantry, jungle, and counterinsurgency tactics; logistical support; military engineering; intelligence; and vehicle, weapons, and communications equipment maintenance. The students, approximately 1,100 each year, come from nineteen Latin American countries. The language of instruction is Spanish.

X

The Ground-Air Conflict

From the American Revolution until today, the U.S. Army has fought in nine major wars and has participated in some 100 lesser conflicts, campaigns, and disturbances of assorted size and shape. The Army has fought in every climate, has maneuvered over every type of terrain, and has engaged enemies of every character and description. But some of the conflicts that have endured longest and have caused deep anguish have been fought on the home front, with the humid Washington jungle constituting the prime battlefield, and the Navy, the Air Force, and even insurgents within the Army's own ranks representing the opponents.

The domestic insurgencies that have rent the Army have already been touched on in this book—the holding actions of the entrenched staff bureaus, the pressures exerted by the reserve components, the assumption by the technical and administrative services of command prerogatives. The conflicts between the Army and its sister services have sprung from competition among all three—rivalry for roles and missions, for a bigger slice of the budget pie, and for manpower. Competition among the services is not necessarily harmful. On the positive side, it prevents complacency, encourages inventiveness, requires critical analysis of the entire military spectrum, and fosters fresh viewpoints while requiring continuing justification for the retention of old ones. These are circumstances that contribute strength and vitality to the military establishment. But to the extent that active rivalry impedes support of one another, permits wastefulness and duplication, and diverts attention from reinforcement of the joint defenses against the common enemy, it is inimicable to the best interests of the nation and of the services themselves. Such a rivalry has been the long-lived, smoldering conflict between the Army and the Air Force over air power. It merits examination because it represents a fundamentally divergent attitude on a matter of overwhelming importance to the Army—and because it is not yet fully resolved.

The Controversy Begins

The military use of the air medium as a factor in warfare seems so distinctly a product of the twentieth century that it generally comes as something of a revelation to learn that the Army's aeronautical operations date back to the mid-nineteenth century. It was in 1861 that the Union Army of the Potomac organized an observation balloon corps and utilized it for battlefield reconnaissance.

Despite employment of observation balloons in the Civil War, and to a much more limited extent in the Spanish-American War, the Army was unimpressed with the performance of the balky, vulnerable gas bags. Military interest in aeronautics became livelier after the Wright brothers made their historic flight. In 1907, the Army created the three-man Aeronautical Division within the Signal Corps to look into the military potential of lighter-than-air craft. The Army purchased a dirigible in 1908; in 1909 it owned its first airplane—a flimsy, 42-mile-an-hour affair—and it proceeded to explore the feasibility of aerial photography and of mounting machine guns on the craft. Five years later, the Aeronautical Division had grown to more than 100 officers and men and boasted an inventory of fifteen planes.

Even then, with aviation so embryonic and feeble a military instrument, the seeds of conflict were being sown. The handful of aviators serving in the Army felt that they were confined and hampered by the limiting nature of their position as a part of the Signal Corps. Complaining that they were being forced to play second fiddle to a range of communications activities, they began to agitate for separate status equal to that of the Signal Corps. Heeding the pleas, Congress in 1914 passed legislation that sought to achieve a compromise. The act established the Aviation Section, which was retained within the Signal Corps structure but which enjoyed greater autonomy than the old Aeronautical Division.

The U.S. Army entered World War I with an air armada of 103 planes—all of them of marginal capability even for those times—and with a force of 1,200 airmen, of whom only 112 were qualified aviators. Massive wartime appropriations expanded this minute organization enormously and rapidly. By the end of the war, U.S. Army aviators had conducted approximately 20,000 flights on pursuit, observation, or bombing missions. Nearly 300 planes had been lost, but this loss was far outweighed by the nearly 800 enemy aircraft shot down. A total of 138 tons of explosives had been dropped on enemy rail, industrial, and troop targets. The air operations had been effective, but they had not been decisive. They had hurt the enemy, but their influence on the outcome of the war had been negligible.

The Army returned from the war with a hard-core group of proponents of air power who saw those 20,000 flights, and especially those 138 tons of explosives, as the turning point of warfare. They saw air power as the key to victory in all future conflicts. But the majority of the Army were not nearly so overwhelmed by the potential of the airplane. They viewed air power as another military weapon—perhaps even as a major weapon of war—but not as a determinant of the outcome of the contest of arms. In their view, the airplane played a supporting role for the conflict on the ground.

Those who subscribed to the "winged victory" belief prosecuted their case vigorously as they sought a stronger voice in shaping military strategy. Their first concrete achievement was Congressional authorization in 1920 for the establishment of the Army Air Service (later renamed the Army Air Corps) independent of the Signal Corps and functioning as a regular combat arm of the Army. In July, 1921, Brigadier General William L. Mitchell, one of the most vocal advocates of air power and a firebrand proponent of an independent air force coequal with the Army and the Navy, received authority to conduct a spectacular demonstration of the potential of military aircraft. Under "Billy" Mitchell's direction, a flight of Army bombers dropped high explosives on the *Ostfriesland,* a captured, well-armored German battleship that had been anchored off the Virginia coast as a target for the test. The bombed battleship sank.

The *Ostfriesland* exploit gained new adherents for the advocates of military air power as the key to victory in war, but it settled nothing. During the 1920's, the airmen continued to remain in the public eye by performing a series of "spectaculars"—long-range flights, speed flights, and endurance flights by means of mid-air refueling. Less spectacularly but more fundamentally, they concentrated with even greater dedication on the evolution of a comprehensive air doctrine. At Langley Field, at Maxwell Field, and at other aviation installations, the airmen immersed themselves in the formation of the principles, concepts, and policies that would shape and direct the air arm. Central to the emerging air doctrine was a bedrock conviction that war henceforth would be fought on one level by traditional surface forces maneuvering inconclusively, and, on a higher level (both literally and figuratively), by the air elements—and that it was on the higher level that war would be pressed to conclusion. Moreover, the dominant opinion among airmen was that the very heart of air power was strategic bombardment with tactical air operations occupying a subordinate position. The bomber, they insisted, would decide the outcome of war. Consequently, to divert air resources to the direct support of the surface fighting would only prolong combat and weaken the ability to assure victory. First priority, the majority of airmen believed, should be accorded to air power in its strategic role, and a lower order of priority should be attached to air power in its supplemental role: support of the "secondary" combat elements, the surface fighting units.

The rest of the Army—meaning the greater portion of it— was slower to realign its doctrine to accommodate the emergence of the airplane as a significant factor in conflict. The ground elements started from the basic position that wars are won or lost on the ground, and that all else is, in the final analysis, a supporting effort. Although the Army did not abandon that position (and still has not) it began to come to grips with the question of the airplane. The initial Army view was that the airplane was another tactical weapons system, like tanks or artillery, and like them should be incorporated into ground tactics to support the war on the ground. Throughout the 1930's, this belief was progressively moderated and enlarged to include a strategic role for air. By the eve of World War II, the official Army view was that the air arm should accord parity to strategic operations and to tactical ground support.

The Breach Widens

Throughout the period that the ground and the air elements had been formulating their separate and divergent doctrines regarding air power, the Army Air Corps had been growing larger, more autonomous, and more restive. Its surge toward independence reached a new high-water mark in mid-1941 when the Army Air Corps was reconstituted as the Army Air Forces. The airmen were now the organizational peers of the ground elements who were, at the same time, collectively designated as the Army Ground Forces. Administratively, this was a sound decision of the Army High Command. The tremendous wartime expansion under way would have been even more difficult to assimilate had the Army not created its three major entities: Army Air Forces (AAF), Army Ground Forces (AGF), and Army Service Forces (ASF). But the division also served to create an organizational framework that encouraged perpetuation and even widening of the doctrinal chasm between the ground and the air arms.

Reorganization of the Army could, and did, segment the establishment into the separate Air, Ground, and Service forces, but no amount of reorganization could eliminate from AGF or ASF the inescapable need for wings of their own. The solution adopted was to create something new—Army Aviation—a sort of clipped-wing, limited-performance flying element consisting of short-range, slow-speed aircraft operating from small, unimproved fields. Army Aviation became an integral part of the ground units in the summer of 1942 with the assignment of ten planes to each infantry division and six to each armored division to serve as aerial observation posts for correcting artillery fire. Very quickly, these unarmed "flying jeeps" were fulfilling such varied, additional missions as battlefield reconnaissance, aerial photography, liaison, and emergency resupply. By the end of the war, Army ground units possessed some 2,000 aircraft, all of them organic to the units like trucks or tanks, and all of the aviators experienced ground-forces officers assigned to ground units like any other technical officer on the roster.

After World War II, several new factors entered upon the scene to complicate the air-ground situation and to exert heavy pressures upon it. The most dramatic of these factors was the atom bomb. With the awesome power of the atom, strategic bombing attained an entirely new magnitude of destructive capability. No one could close his eyes to the mushroom cloud.

Hard on the heels of the atom bomb came the National Security Act of 1947. Under the terms of the act, the Department of the Air Force and the U.S. Air Force now came into being as coequals of the Department of the Army and the U.S. Army. The vision that "Billy" Mitchell and his small group of devoted adherents had embraced in the 1920's—an independent Air Force—had now become a reality. The long-sought goal had finally been reached.

One final post-World War II development affected the situation—the new national strategy. The basic strategic concept adopted by the nation during this period was one of nuclear deterrence and, that failing, of massive nuclear retaliation. Those who framed the national policies conceived of the next war as a short, violent nuclear exchange. This concept represented a complete convergence of national policy with the belief long ascendant among airmen that strategic bombing was the key to victory.

These three elements—the atom bomb, the independence of the Air Force, and the adoption of a national policy that placed primary reliance upon a massive nuclear retaliatory capability—created the conditions under which the combat requirements of the Army were neglected. Now the Air Force was completely free to concentrate on enlarging and improving its strategic bombing capacity, and it proceeded to do so. The Army urged that greater emphasis be placed on the two areas in which it was dependent upon the Air Force—tactical air support for ground operations and strategic airlift for ground forces—but its pleas were largely unheeded. To keep the situation in proper perspective, two facts must be pointed out. First, the Air Force acted from conviction, not from pique or animosity toward the Army, and it acted in complete conformity with the national will. Second, the Army prosecuted its case with a timidity and a lack of aggressiveness that served its cause poorly; it should have had a little more "Billy Mitchellism" in its make-up.

The Awakening

Those who framed the national strategy were proven wrong at 0400 hours on June 25, 1950, when North Korean combat elements attacked across the 38th parallel. The Korean War was a conventional conflict—but a particularly nasty one. It was a war in which strategic bombing played no role of any great consequence, in which nuclear retaliation was never an issue, in which the Army—on whose shoulders the greatest burden of the combat fell—sorely needed tactical air support that it often failed to receive adequately. The role of Army Aviation assumed heightened significance, and the Army's air fleet grew to approximately double its World War II size. Army aviators, flying short-range fixed and rotary-wing planes, performed all of their earlier missions plus such new ones as battlefield casualty evacuation, rapid deployment of weapons systems, and serving as airborne radio relay stations. The Air Force was well aware of the growing Army air fleet and it was not pleased with the prospect, but, under the circumstances, it could hardly complain loudly.

Korea demonstrated that conventional wars had not been outmoded by the atom bomb. If anything, conventional warfare had become a more likely alternate to the suicidal madness of nuclear holocaust. And now a second alternate became prominent as the Communist bloc commenced to exhibit a mounting fondness for "wars of national liberation" and insurgencies. This, too, was primarily ground conflict far removed from the atom bomb and only peripherally linked to strategic bombing with non-nuclear devices. It was clear that the monolithic view of war as an all-or-nothing affair—nuclear exchange or nuclear stalemate—was a strategic strait jacket. It was too restraining a concept, too confining. It denied freedom of choice and of action, and it failed to recognize the very real menace of conventional and unconventional conflict.

To meet the changed nature of the threat, the national strategy expanded from the inflexibility of massive strategic retaliation within a nuclear context to a more realistic, more flexible strategy that permitted options and graduated levels of response tailored to the nature of the provocation. For the Army, this strategy meant forward deployment of tactical units, creation of an unconventional warfare capability, and development of greater mobility. For the Air Force, it meant expansion and enhancement of its capabilities for tactical support for ground operations and creation of adequate capacity for the strategic lift of surface units.

The breach between the ground and air elements had been costly. The Air Force, planning for a short, nuclear war, had failed to maintain a large modern carrier fleet equal to the strategic deployment requirements of the Army. The tactical arm of the Air Force had been developed as a secondary effort, subordinate to USAF's strategic bombing capability, and subordination had prevented it from realizing its full potential. There was a dangerous imbalance between what the Army required of the Air Force and what the Air Force was in a position to deliver.

Aggravating the entire situation was the fact that the Army and the Air Force had followed their separate paths for so long that it was no simple task to have them link arms and march in cadence. For too long, their doctrinal approaches had been developed independently of each other, and, for too long, each had been preparing for a different kind of war. As a result, there was a broad inconsistency between their concepts, an incompatibility between their equipment and resources, a lack of a really discriminating appreciation of each other's needs and potentials, and a minimum of joint experience in meaningful, cooperative training and in the development of common procedures. These were conditions that could not be overcome overnight. Remedying the defects accumulated over a period of years required time, energy, money, suppression of parochialism, innovation and testing, good will, and good sense. But, whatever the shortcomings and whatever the difficulties in rectifying them, the most important first steps had been taken: The problems had been identified and acknowledged, and remedies were being sought.

The Remedies

A major remedy adopted was the invigoration of the unified command system and the creation of new unified combatant commands. By assigning a single commander for all of the service components allocated to a specific area of responsibility, an operational framework for coordination and mutual support was provided. Moreover, since all of the unified combatant commands receive their orders directly from the Joint Chiefs of Staff, where the views of all the Services are presented and evaluated, there is no opportunity for the individual services to dilute or "interpret" the instructions en route between the Joint Chiefs and the commands. Thus, all of the components within a given unified command are preparing cooperatively to fight the same kind of war and are jointly developing their operational procedures. Of the unified combatant commands, the one that came straight out of the ground-air breach, and the one that contributes most directly to healing that wound, is the U.S. Strike Command. USSTRICOM, because it welds virtually all combat-ready Army divisions and Air Force tactical air wings in reserve in the continental United States into a single entity, creates the ground-air team that must exist for success on a battlefield that is inescapably tridimensional. Within the framework of USSTRICOM, the ground and air tactical elements are training together and are developing recommended joint doctrine that exploits the strengths of each and recognizes the limitations of each. The consequence of such combined training experience and of the growing reciprocal understanding between the ground and the air components of USSTRICOM are bound to have a salutary effect on the Army and the Air Force as a whole.

To provide adequate strategic airlift capacity, the entire air fleet has been thoroughly overhauled. New carriers of greater range, greater capacity, and greater speed were procured in quantity while the phase-out of obsolescent craft was begun. Prominent in the air carrier fleet today are the highly effective C-141—a 550-mile-an-hour jet with a range of 3,500 miles carrying a 40-ton load—the C-135, and the C-130. But bigger and better things are in the offing. The first eight C-5A aircraft were scheduled for procurement in 1967, with greatly augmented procurement scheduled for 1968, and the first one is to be delivered in 1969. A monster of a plane twice the size of any currently in the Air Force inventory, it will carry two columns of trucks loaded side by side; one dozen C-5A's could have handled the entire Berlin airlift, which required more than 300 C-54's. Highly important from the Army's point of view are the C-5A's rapid, "drive-through" loading feature and its ability to operate from short, low-strength airfields, which permits routine delivery of troops and cargo well forward in a theater of operations.

Another development of surpassing significance has been the marked expansion of the tactical elements of the Army and the Air Force so that each now has far more substantial resources to contribute to the ground-air team. From 1961 until 1966, tactical air wings in the Air Force increased from sixteen to twenty-four, while active Army divisions went from fourteen to seventeen. For the Air Force, this has meant an impressive 50 per cent augmentation of its basic tactical units and, for the Army, a not inconsiderable 20 per cent augmentation.

Apart from the expansion of the numbers of the tactical ground and air units, but nevertheless related to it, is the collateral growth of Army Aviation. The Army's organic air fleet has now grown to 8,000 planes and by 1968 is expected to approach 10,000. While the Army aircraft still conform to an "Army configuration" that makes them noncompetitive with the Air Force's planes and enables them to perform ground support missions that the Air Force is not equipped or trained to render, they are far superior in performance to the craft in the Army's inventory a dozen years ago. No longer are they all unarmed "sitting ducks"; many are outfitted with machine guns, rockets, and even air-to-ground missiles for delivery of suppressive fire.

The basic question of the Army's possessing any aircraft at all—a circumstance that has been a thorn in the side of the Air Force in the past—was settled in 1966 by an agreement between the two services that clearly confirmed the Army's right to maintain its own air fleet for ground-force missions. The agreement bars Army Aviation from operating fixed-wing planes for intratheater lift of troops and from developing aircraft designed either for deep probes into enemy air space or for air-to-air combat. Thus, Army Aviation will remain largely, but not exclusively, a helicopter force. Army fixed-wing planes will be restricted primarily to command, administrative, and inspection missions. Army helicopters will continue to provide tactical lift, reconnaissance and surveillance, weapons redeployment, emergency resupply, medical evacuation, service support, and liaison missions on the battlefield.

The Army–Air Force agreement has not settled for all time all of the problem areas that grow out of the Army's justifiable insistence on flapping its own wings. The major remaining source of potential friction surrounds the matter of VTOL (vertical take-off and landing) aircraft. These hybrid craft require no runway, since they have the ability to take off or land vertically like helicopters; yet, in level flight, they achieve speeds within the range of fixed-wing planes. These flight characteristics can be achieved in different ways, but the most promising seems to be a tilt-wing configuration that swivels the power plants to provide vertical thrust for take-off and landing and horizontal thrust for level flight. The Air Force has a direct interest in VTOL craft. But to an even greater extent, VTOL is applicable to ground force operations, because, at 300 miles per hour in level flight—a speed readily attainable by VTOL craft—planes are virtually immune to small-arms fire from the ground, and because that speed and the vertical take-off and landing characteristics offer the kind of flexibility and mobility that are required by ground forces on the modern battlefield. For the Army, VTOL promises to be a superior vehicle for delivering fire support for battlefield maneuver and for tactical airlift.

The Army–Air Force agreement is cognizant of the fact that each service has a stake in VTOL, and it acknowledges the right of each to proceed with development. Therein lie the acorns that could grow into oaks of conflict when the Army and the Air Force vie for funds for development and procurement of VTOL craft. Moreover, there is a possibility that once both services have integrated VTOL's in their inventories, they may find themselves in competition for missions and roles for the craft.

The VTOL conflict, if it should come, lies in the future. For the present, a refreshing spirit of cooperation and intelligent, mutual effort is at last evident in the ground-air team. It is a promising start to what it is hoped will prove to be eventual and complete elimination of the rupture that has victimized the Army for decades.

XI

The Reserve Forces

The Army has three parts: the Regular Army (or the "Active Army," as it is sometimes termed today), the Army National Guard, and the Army Reserve. Each is a component of the Army establishment; jointly, the three constitute the Army of the United States. The Pentagon likes to speak of the Army's "oneness," but there is sometimes more pious hope than unquestioned belief in the actuality of the description.

The less than perfect harmony among the components of the Army has substantial historic precedent. The twofold concept of both a full-time and a part-time soldiery grew out of disagreement over the type of military force the United States should have. The decision to maintain both types was a compromise that, for a long time, failed to satisfy implacable partisans of one or the other view and that, until recent years, was aggravated by a marked disparity in the general levels of training, leadership, equipment, and operational concept of the active and the reserve organizations.

Although, to be sure, militiamen have performed heroically and with great professional competence throughout the history of the republic, there have been enough instances of militia failure to cause a breach with the soldiers of the Regular Army—one not fully healed until the twentieth century. One such example was the Battle of Queenston Heights. In that battle, fought on October 13, 1812, a militia general, Stephen Van Rensselaer, commanded 3,500 New York militiamen and 450 Regulars facing an inferior Canadian force across the

Niagara River. Van Rensselaer decided to attack across the water. He had few boats available for the crossing to the Canadian side, but by loading them to capacity he was able to dispatch half his Regulars to the far bank, where they charged and secured the heights. The dislodged Canadians regrouped and counterattacked. Badly outnumbered and unreinforced from the main body, the Regulars were in an extremely precarious position, and Van Rensselaer, vacillating, did nothing to aid them. His militiamen, loudly proclaiming that they had enlisted only to repel invaders and not to fight beyond New York's borders, lined the shore to watch the slaughter of the desperate Regulars, like spectators at a bullfight. Immediately after the debacle, Van Rensselaer resigned his militia commission, but his act of contrition did not erase Queenston Heights from the record.

By World War I, sweeping changes had been wrought. Of eight U.S. divisions in that war rated excellent or superior by the German Supreme Command, six were National Guard. In the same war, 43 per cent of all the officers serving in the U.S. Army were Reservists. In World War II and in the various crises since then, the reserve components of the Army have demonstrated a degree of professionalism and competence that have earned the full respect of the Regulars. Today, the three components of the Army are judged by the same criteria and must each attain the same standards.

The National Guard

Of the three components of the Army, the National Guard has the longest continuous history, tracing its lineage back to the militia units, or "train bands," formed by seventeenth-century American settlers for their self-protection. The basic concept, then as now, was of a part-time soldiery, an organization of citizen-soldiers who would leap to the defense of the nation in time of emergency. This concept was formalized in Article I, Section 8, of the United States Constitution, which empowered Congress to call out the militia "to execute the Laws of the

Union, suppress insurrections, and repel Invasions," and which authorized Congress to provide for "organizing, arming, and disciplining, the Militia, and for governing such Part of them as may be employed in the Service of the United States, reserving to the States respectively, the Appointment of the Officers and the Authority of training the Militia according to the discipline prescribed by Congress." However, Congress failed to prescribe the "discipline" and this failure, coupled with the right of each state to organize, train, and administer its separate militia to suit itself, led to a lack of coherence, uniformity, and effectiveness. Many higher-ranking officers were political appointees distinguished by military ineptitude. Company grade officers were elected by the militiamen themselves, and the majority vote was usually garnered by the candidate who could belt his drinks or his rivals with equal dispatch—attributes not necessarily related to military ability.

A small beginning in enhancing the federal government's influence over the militia was made in 1808 when Congress inaugurated a system of subsidies to the states for support of their militias. And a psychological advance was achieved in 1824 when a New York militia regiment adopted the name "National Guard" as an expression of recognition of the Revolutionary War contributions of the Marquis de Lafayette, a former commander of the French *Garde Nationale*. By 1900, most state militias had assumed the National Guard title. The new designation did not correct the flaws of the militia system, but it did at least inject a certain flavor of implied federalism throughout the organization.

Hampered by the various defects under which they operated, the militiamen served the nation spottily—sometimes extremely well, sometimes poorly—throughout the nineteenth century. The first really significant move to eliminate the handicaps that limited the effectiveness of the militia system came in 1903 with Congressional passage of the Dick Act, which defined state and federal responsibilities and redesignated the active militia as the "Organized Militia" of the United States.

Each state was allocated responsibility for furnishing manpower and armory facilities for its militia units. The federal government was allotted responsibility for training, equipping, and paying the troops. Provision was made for War Department inspections of Organized Militia units and for joint Regular Army–Organized Militia training exercises. Congress also stipulated that in the event a state failed to maintain appropriate training standards for its units, the federal government would withhold its appropriations for Organized Militia support within the offending state. The level of training and of leadership within the militia very quickly reflected a marked improvement under the stimulus of the various provisions of the Dick Act.

A later Congressional action, the National Defense Act of 1916, as amended, adopted "National Guard" as the official designation for the militia, empowered the federal regulation of standards for commission and enlistment, and established an organizational structure that conformed to that of the Regular Army. The act of 1916 also established the National Guard as a component of the nation's peacetime military structure and, when in active federal service, as a part of the Army of the United States. But the most significant provision of the 1916 legislation was to create a new authority under which the President could direct the National Guard to serve under federal command. Since 1792, under the Constitution, the President had enjoyed the right to "call" the National Guard into active service to enforce federal laws, suppress insurrection, and repel invasions. Under a call, today as in the past, National Guard troops are subject to Presidential orders and to all Army regulations, but they retain state identities, and the respective state governors continue to appoint and promote the officers. The new law granted the President the right to "draft" or "order" the National Guard into federal service upon a declaration of war. Under an "order" into federal service, the National Guard severs all connections with the states, thus suspending all effective influence of the individual governors.

In 1933, an amendment to the National Defense Act of 1916 created a new entity, the National Guard of the United States (NGUS), as a reserve component of the Army. The NGUS was composed of the National Guard of the separate states. When not on active duty with the Army, the Guard units were to retain their state identities; when federalized, the units would assume their NGUS identity as a federal reserve and, until their return to state status, the separate states would not possess National Guard units of their own. A major provision of the amendment granted the President the authority to order the NGUS to active duty whenever Congress declared a national emergency, without going through state governors.

The National Guard of the United States was ordered into federal service in late 1940 to cope with the emergency situation that preceded U.S. entrance into World War II. More than 300,000 guardsmen served during the war, bringing to the battlefield eighteen effective divisions and scores of nondivisional units.

Following World War II, the National Guard was reorganized and further strengthened. In 1947, to conform to the establishment of the separate U.S. Air Force, the air units of the National Guard were spun off to form the Air National Guard, while the ground units were redesignated the Army National Guard. Both the Air and the Army National Guards come under the jurisdiction of the National Guard Bureau, which is an agency of both the Army and the Air Force. Within the Army staff, the National Guard Bureau operates under the supervision of the Chief, Office of Reserve Components. (See Chart 6.) The bureau is staffed by Regular and National Guard personnel of both the Army and the Air Force. The bureau chief is appointed by the President from among National Guard candidates proposed by the state governors, and the post is usually alternated between a ground officer and an air officer. The bureau advises the Departments of the Army and of the Air Force on National Guard matters, assists in the formulation and administration of programs for the Guard, and serves as the channel between the departments and the states on National Guard business. Within each state, supervision and administration of the state's military forces are conducted by the State National Guard Headquarters. The senior officer in the state headquarters is the adjutant general, appointed by the governor and serving as his military adviser.

In 1954, the Army National Guard was assigned its first active peacetime federal mission: participation in the air defense of the United States. Currently, operating under the control of the U.S. Army Air Defense Command, Army National Guard units man more than one-third of the Nike-Hercules air-defense sites in the continental United States and all of the Nike-Hercules sites in Hawaii. These Guard units serve full-time but remain in state status.

Today, the Army National Guard has a strength of approximately 400,000, divided among 4,000 units in the 50 states, Puerto Rico, and the District of Columbia; of some 25 National Guard divisions; 8 could be fully operational alongside Regular Army divisions in as little as 4 to 8 weeks. The National Guard mission continues to have a twofold character. In its Federal status, it provides trained units and qualified individuals for active duty in time of war or national emergency; in its state role, it provides organized units to protect life and property and to preserve order.

The Army Reserve

The concept of a reserve force dates back to colonial America, but as a U.S. Army component in being, the Army Reserve is a relatively modern innovation. The idea is rooted in the same citizen-soldier philosophy that led to the creation of the National Guard. Early advocates of a reserve force envisioned it as a trained, organized supplement to the Regular Army that would be national in character and undiluted by affiliation with the separate states. However, the state militia view, with its inherent defects, prevailed. Partisans of a national reserve force were thwarted, and many years were to pass before a reserve organization free of state ties was established.

The first official designation of a reserve force occurred in 1866 when President Andrew Johnson signed into law a bill that defined the U.S. Army as consisting of 45 infantry regiments, 10 cavalry regiments, and 4 artillery regiments, with 4 of the infantry regiments—composed of men wounded in combat—constituting a limited-duty "Veterans' Reserve Corps." But this, of course, was a totally different sort of organization from today's Army Reserve concept.

As a modern component of the Army, the Reserve started in 1908, with Congressional creation of the Medical Reserve Corps of the Army. This organization was expanded by legislation in 1912, 1916, 1920, and by later Congressional action, until it gradually assumed its present identity as the United States Army Reserve (USAR). Until fairly recently, its chief purpose was to provide trained Reservists, mostly officers, to bring Regular Army and National Guard units to full wartime strength in periods of emergency. In that respect, it was a structure of individuals rather than units. Such units as did exist were largely "paper" organizations that were maintained at far-below-normal strength and, thus, at far-below-required levels of effectiveness. The contribution of the Reserve to the total military strength of the nation was in its individual manpower, not in its units. The significance of the Reserve as a source of combat leaders was illustrated during World War II when a survey of 5 divisions revealed that 52 per cent of the lieutenant colonels, 83 per cent of the majors, and 70 per cent of the captains were Reservists.

The character of the USAR changed radically during the 1950's, in large measure because of the passage of the Reserve Forces Act of 1955. This law provided that every man liable for military service thereafter could choose various combinations of active duty and Reserve training of either six or eight years' duration. Most chose to combine their service, with a portion of the obligated period on active duty and the remainder in either the USAR or in the National Guard. Thus, since 1955, the Army Reserve has been assured of a constant input of trained enlisted men, enabling it to grow into an effective force of some 3,000 combat and combat-support units, plus a large pool of experienced individual reinforcements. Approximately three of every four Reserve units are now classified as "Immediate Reserve"; that is to say, they are trained, organized, equipped, and manned so as to be immediately available in the event of mobilization.

The major source of officers for the Army is the Reserve Officers Training Corps. The ROTC had its genesis in 1819 when the American Literary, Scientific, and Military Academy (later to become Norwich University) was founded in Vermont. That school was the first American institution of higher learning, other than West Point, to prescribe military studies as a part of the curriculum. It was followed by the establishment of other military colleges and academies and, eventually, by a system of Federal support for colleges that included military science and tactics in their curricula. The National Defense Act of 1916 regularized and formalized the concept by creating the Reserve Officers Training Corps as a framework for the program conducted in the schools. Currently, ROTC operates as a four-year program in nine military colleges and nearly 250 civilian colleges and universities. In addition, the ROTC Vitalization Act of 1964 established a two-year program for students unable to participate in ROTC during their freshman and sophomore years.

About 12,000 cadets annually are granted Reserve commissions as second lieutenants upon successful completion of the four-year ROTC program. Of this number, some 1,000 are designated "distinguished military graduates" and are tendered appointments in the Regular Army. About 85 per cent of all second lieutenants and about 45 per cent of all officers regardless of grade on active duty today are ROTC graduates.

At Department of the Army level, over-all responsibility for both the Army Reserve and the Army and the National Guard programs, and for the formulation of pertinent plans and policies, is vested in the Chief of the Office of Reserve Components, a member of the General Staff. The Deputy Chief of Staff for Personnel is responsible for the conduct of the Reserve Officers Training Corps program. (See Chart 6.)

The Future of the Reserve Components

Present Pentagon planning indicates that more changes are in store for the reserve components, both the Army Reserve and the National Guard. Change is inevitable as the Army leadership strives to evolve the best possible format for the force structure that supplements the Regular Army and that provides the Army establishment with ready expandability. The objective of current planning is to delineate clearly between the National Guard and the Reserve so that the two components are nonduplicating and noncompetitive, and so that each is fully compatible with the other and with the needs of the Army as a whole. The ultimate intent is to realign the two components in such a way that the National Guard becomes the parent of all Army units not on active service, while the USAR becomes the parent of all individual reserve component personnel not affiliated with a unit. This would be a return to the traditional roles of each—the National Guard as a source of trained units and the Army Reserve as a source of trained individuals for reinforcement of units.

The first steps in this direction have already been taken. During 1965, 750 Reserve units considered superfluous to the Army's projected requirements were eliminated, their equipment was reallocated to National Guard units, and their manpower was redistributed to the National Guard and to the Army Reserve mobilization pool of individual reinforcements. These actions permit maintaining Guard units at a higher level of combat readiness, maintaining the Reserve in closer conformity to the individual reinforcement needs of the Army establishment, and simplifying the administration of the reserve component structure. If all the current planning were put into effect, the over-all total of eliminated units of various sizes would run to more than 2,000, but the remaining units—8 divisions, 11 separate brigades, the "on-site" air defense battalions operating with ARADCOM, and the assorted support and service units—would be operated on a priority basis affording them the manning, the equipment, and the training to achieve readiness-for-deployment goals of approximately 8 weeks. In addition to all other benefits that would accrue from the realignment of the reserve structure, the streamlined setup would be expected to produce annual savings of about $150 million.

The proposed changes in the mission and organization of the Army's reserve components seem so logical that there should be little resistance to them. But such is not the case. Congress, whose blessings are required to carry out all the proposed changes, has exhibited a reluctance to approve the plans in their entirety. This reluctance stems from at least two sources. The first is a belief that the national defense is better served by retention of reserve units that are completely federal in character, as in the Army Reserve, rather than depending solely on reserve units that have a dual state-federal character, as in the National Guard—despite all of the legal provisions for federal employment of the Guard and all of the requirements for the Guard to adhere to federal standards. The second is the opposition of Army Reserve partisans who are reluctant to see organized units disappear from the Reserve, viewing such a move as a downgrading and weakening of the component. In the meantime, the Army is introducing such realignments as are possible pending the granting of a Congressional go-ahead.

XII

The Army and the Congress

Determined to insure civilian ascendancy over the military, the framers of the Constitution left no room for doubting that the Army and the Congress were destined for a close and continuing relationship. All agencies of the executive branch are subject to scrutiny by Congress and to a measure of legislative control over their operations, but none so fully as the military. This is implicit in Article I, Section 8, of the Constitution, which provides:

> The Congress shall have Power To . . . provide for the common Defence . . . of the United States; . . . To declare War . . . ; To raise and support Armies . . . ; To make Rules for the Government and Regulation of the land and naval Forces; . . . To provide for organizing, arming, and disciplining, the Militia, and for governing such Part of them as may be employed in the Service of the United States . . .

This broad Constitutional mandate for Congressional oversight of military affairs provides the framework within which the Congress is empowered—indeed, required—to shape the character of the armed forces. But even more than that, it is clear that the armed forces are creatures of the Congress, dependent upon that body for their very existence.

Congressional influence over military affairs is pervasive. Even in technical military matters where Congress possesses no specific authority to intervene, it has the means to bring its full weight to bear. For example, the express military powers accorded to Congress do not include the right to make operational military decisions of a purely technical nature. However, a "strong" Congress can influence such decisions by withholding funds for specific items of hardware, by altering manpower allocations, or by realignment of roles and missions among the armed forces. In effect, there is virtually no facet of the Army or of its sister services that is completely immune to Congressional leverage.

For the century and a half preceding passage of the "Unification" Act of 1947, the House and Senate each maintained two military committees—one with responsibility for Army matters and the second for Navy matters. Following passage of the act and its creation of an independent Air Force, the separate committees were consolidated into a single armed services committee in each chamber. These two committees are charged with overall administration of Congress' broad responsibilities in military affairs. Other committees, however, also have a direct interest in the military as it relates to their spheres of activity—for example, the appropriations committees on budgetary matters, the public works committees on civil construction performed by the Corps of Engineers, and the foreign affairs committees on the military aid portions of the foreign aid bills. Furthermore, each of these bodies has subcommittees that may from time to time be concerned with military affairs, and either chamber of Congress may create special, temporary investigating bodies to deal with specific aspects of the armed forces. Because so many committees are concerned with military matters either exclusively or peripherally, and because so much of Congress' work is performed within the committee format, at each legislative session there is a constant parade of military witnesses to testify at hearings.

Increasingly, especially in the post–World War II years, Congress, acting through its committees, has required the armed forces to explain, to justify, or to defend their actions and contemplated actions. Military accountability to Congress is entirely consistent with the American system of governmental checks and balances. Beyond that, it serves the vital purposes of exposing errors of judgment or of execution by the military, and of stimulating corrective action. But sometimes the preventive medicine of accountability to Congress can be a bitter pill for the military to swallow, not because they resent examination and medication, but because the doctors handling the case may not always be suited to the occupation. This is a consequence of Congressional "seniority," whereby committee members (and their chairmen) assume their post simply because they have been on Capitol Hill a long time and not because they are necessarily well qualified to treat the military. Not only has Congress a statutory obligation to oversee the armed forces, it also has a moral obligation to the electorate to investigate fully and legislate wisely where defense of the nation is at issue. Committee hearings are critically important to the effective discharge of these responsibilities, but any hearing conducted by a political body is a particularly sensitive instrument that must be wielded with restraint, wisdom, and objectivity. A member in need of headlines to bolster his chances of re-election, or one with a score to settle, can, if he chooses, misuse a committee hearing as a partisan forum and a political weapon—as the lamentable Army-McCarthy hearings of 1954 so vividly demonstrated.

Sometimes a hearing before a committee can develop into a contest of wills. Such was the case in the 1965 hearing concerning the so-called Reserve Merger plan announced by Secretary of Defense Robert S. McNamara. The plan was conceived as a means of improving efficiency and economy by eliminating virtually all units of the Army Reserve, leaving it composed primarily of individual Reservists, with the National Guard the component of organized units not on active duty. The Senate Armed Services Committee, disapproving the plan, "requested" that it be held in abeyance for at least one year. Late in 1965, Secretary McNamara, avoiding fanfare and any reference to a Reserve forces "merger," announced the elimination of 751 Army Reserve units, thus substituting a flanking action for a frontal assault. Predictably, Congress reacted volubly. The chairman of the House Armed Services Committee summed it up succinctly when he said the action "probably is legal, but it isn't the intent of Congress." The character and the performance of the Army can be shaped by Congressional "intent" as well as by legislative decision, the Constitutional authority of the Commander in Chief and the adroitness of the military leadership notwithstanding.

There is a continuing and voluminous interchange between Congress and the military. The appearance of witnesses before committees is only a part of the whole. Individual Congressmen make direct requests to the Pentagon for additional data to assist them in formulating their positions on pending legislation; such requests must be handled expeditiously and responsively. In addition, members of Congress are in constant communication with the armed forces over problems involving their constituents. These problems range from the injured outcry by businessmen over the phasing-out of a local military installation to the anguished plea from a mother who has not received mail from her soldier son. Despite the wide variety of the military-connected matters disturbing the people back home, one common denominator links all constituents: they are voters. Since votes are the staff of life for Congressmen, they are energetic in passing these problems on to the Pentagon for solution. In an average year, the Army might receive some 60,000 letters, 75,000 telephone calls, and 7,500 personal visits from Congressmen. To control and service these approaches and to supervise over-all Army-Congress relations, the Secretary of the Army maintains the office of Chief of Legislative Liaison.

The Chief of Legislative Liaison, a general officer, advises the Secretary and the Chief of Staff of all Congressional developments affecting the Army and of the legislative implications of all Army activities, conceives and controls Army programs involving relations with Capitol Hill, and is responsible for liaison between the Army and Congress. (But the Comptroller of the Army is responsible for dealing with Congress where budgets and appropriations are involved, and the Chief of Engineers deals with Congress on matters pertaining to civil works.) To assist him, the Chief of Legislative Liaison has a staff of about 100, one-third of them uniformed personnel. Most of the staff is located at the Pentagon, but small sections are also maintained at the Senate and House office buildings. (See Chart 7.)

The Army is not merely reactive to Congressional stimulus in its contacts with that body—it also initiates proposals for military legislation by Congress. This is a long, intricate, and tedious process that is supervised by the Chief of Legislative Liaison. Every legislative proposal originating within the Army must be painstakingly researched and analyzed to insure that it is sound and that it says exactly what is intended—no more and no less. This is not quite so simple a task as it might seem. An example of the complications facing all the services occurred a few years ago when the Navy proposed an innocuous bill to repeal an earlier law designating the Marine Corps ration, and to substitute a new ration. After the requested legislation was voted by Congress, the Navy discovered to its dismay that a rider tacked onto the repealed law had contained the authority for creating the post of the Chief of the Bureau of Yards and Docks. In improving the Marine diet, the Navy had inadvertently lost an admiral. (He had to operate by dispensation of Congress until the error could be rectified.)

After the Chief of Legislative Liaison is satisfied that the proposed bill is sound and will achieve the desired results, it must be coordinated with all appropriate segments of the Army, with the other armed forces, with the Department of Defense, with the Bureau of the Budget, and with any other government agency that might be affected. If the proposal survives all these hurdles, it is then submitted to the Speaker of the House and the President of the Senate. But the legislative liaison job is not yet finished—Army witnesses must be provided to furnish supporting testimony, and the bill itself must be monitored carefully to insure that no crippling amendments are added in

Chart 7
ORGANIZATION OF THE OFFICE, CHIEF OF LEGISLATIVE LIAISON (OCLL)

CHIEF OF LEGISLATIVE LIAISON

Formulates, coordinates, and supervises policies and programs concerning the Army's relations with Congress and is responsible for liaison between the Army and Congress except with the appropriations committees in areas affecting budgets and appropriations and except for Corps of Engineers, civil functions, and Civil Defense.

Advises Secretary of the Army and Chief of Staff of Congressional developments affecting the Army and on legislative aspects of Army policies, plans, and programs.

SPECIAL ASSISTANT FOR LEGISLATIVE AFFAIRS

Maintains close relations between Department of Army and key committees and members of Congress. Provides advice and counsel on legislative matters with which the Army is concerned.

EXECUTIVE

Manages and coordinates all activities of the OCLL. Synthesizes reports on Congressional attitudes. Monitors and reports on selected Congressional hearings of interest to Army. Coordinates the travel of members and committees of Congress on matters of Army interest.

ADMINISTRATIVE OFFICE

Responsible for OCLL administrative activities, including the preparation of correspondence, reports, personnel, budgetary, travel and supply matters.

Serves as office of records. Maintains central file, mail and message center facilities.

Administers internal security program.

SENATE LIAISON DIVISION

Maintains and operates office in the Senate Office Building to provide Army liaison service to the members and the committees of the Senate.

Assists Congress in understanding policies, actions, operations, and requirements of the Army.

Replies to inquiries and to matters referred to the Army for resolution.

Analyzes Congressional trends and problems and advises OCLL and the Army staff on the status of Congressional relations.

HOUSE LIAISON DIVISION

Maintains and operates office in the House Office Building to provide Army liaison service to the members and the committees of the House of Representatives.

Assists Congress in understanding policies, actions, operations, and requirements of the Army.

Replies to inquiries and to matters referred to the Army for resolution.

Analyzes Congressional trends and problems and advises OCLL and the Army staff on the status of Congressional relations.

CONGRESSIONAL INQUIRY DIVISION

Replies to inquiries received from members and committees of Congress and their staffs regarding specific individual personnel actions and Army personnel policies pertaining to individuals.

Advises Chief of Legislative Liaison and the appropriate Army staff agencies regarding trends of Congressional personnel inquiries.

SPECIAL OPERATIONS DIVISION

Replies to inquiries received from members and committees of Congress and their staffs regarding policies and actions of the Army in the fields of military operations, installations, logistics, Reserve components, and military and civilian personnel policies.

Provides information to members and committees of Congress on Army activities pertaining to a state, Congressional district, or geographic area.

Monitors and coordinates with DOD and Department of Army actions in the above areas and advises Chief of Legislative Liaison.

LEGISLATIVE DIVISION

Monitors and reports on legislative actions of the Congress of interest to the Army.

Coordinates and supervises the DOD legislative program within the Department of Army. Processes and coordinates other legislative proposals of interest to the Army.

Coordinates with Department of Army and DOD staff agencies and with Congressional committees the preparation for, monitoring, and reporting of hearings before Congressional committees, except annual posture and authorization hearings before the Armed Services committees. Provides counsel and advice for Army witnesses who testify before these committees.

CONGRESSIONAL INVESTIGATIONS DIVISION

Monitors and reports on investigative actions of the Congress of interest to the Army.

Replies to inquiries received from investigative committees of the Congress.

Coordinates the preparation for investigative hearings before Congressional committees with appropriate Department of Army and DOD staff agencies and provides counsel and advice for Army witnesses who testify before these committees.

PLANS AND PROJECTS DIVISION

Maintains contact with the Army staff and participates in Department of Army planning activities to ensure consideration of Congressional implications. Keeps OCLL informed of the status of Department of Army basic policies and plans.

Prepares and maintains plans as required to implement Department of Army legislative liaison programs.

Coordinates with Department of Army and DOD staff agencies and with Congressional committees the preparation for, monitoring, and reporting of hearings for which assigned responsibility, including the annual posture and authorization hearings before the Armed Services committees. Reviews and analyzes the Congressional Record and other Congressional publications.

either chamber. The entire process from origination of the proposal within the Army until passage of the legislation rarely takes less than two years and sometimes stretches into five or six.

The same degree of care that the Army accords its own legislative proposals must also be devoted to those originating in other government agencies or in the Congress itself in order to determine, prior to passage, what implications they might hold for the Army. During a recent session of Congress, a Treasury-sponsored bill was introduced for consideration; under its provisions, the Department of Justice would have been granted the right to try Treasury Department employees for certain offenses. A careful reading of the bill in the Pentagon revealed that the wording was such that it would have the unintended additional effect of granting the Justice Department jurisdiction over military personnel for all offenses except absence without leave. When this effect was pointed out to Congress, the wording was altered suitably.

In a relatively short time, the Army will round out its second century as a creature of Congress, looking to Capitol Hill for enabling legislation and for operating funds. In all the years that have passed, the Army has learned that Congress can be both objective and partisan, generous and penurious, discerning and groping, deliberate and impulsive. Despite the fact that Congress may at times be contradictory in the manner in which it faces up to its military responsibilities, there is no doubt that it does face up to those obligations fully and attempts to discharge them as it thinks best. In its relations with Congress, the Army conceives one of its dominant functions to be to sway the thinking of Congress to fit the pattern that the Army considers best. Ultimately, the interplay between Congress and the Army becomes translated into a defense structure that is reasonable for the times, taking into consideration all of the needs of the nation.

XIII

The Road Ahead

In following the U.S. Army along its almost two-centuries-old route of march, pausing now and then to explore some of the more significant twists and turns in the torturous trail, this book has given special attention to conditions and circumstances of the Army today. But the long march is not ended. The trail winds on, and the Army is continually in the process of breaking camp to set out on it. What lies ahead? What problems and changes can be predicted with reasonable assurance of accuracy? What kind of Army is the United States likely to have five, ten, twenty years from now?

Nowhere in the Army's vast inventory of matériel are there any crystal balls. No Army TOE provides for a fortuneteller. Nobody can perceive the Army's future with infallible clarity, nor does clairvoyance merit a part in any projection of the Army. Yet, the Army must plan and prepare for the future; it must attempt to pierce the mist shrouding the trail ahead or it risks fighting tomorrow's wars without the benefit of tomorrow's weapons and concepts. The result, at best, could be limited success. At worst, it could be utter failure.

How can the Army prepare itself to cope with circumstances that have not yet come to pass, with situations that have yet to develop, with problems whose dimensions and whose nature have yet to be identified?

It would be both futile and dangerous for any army to assume that yesterday's wars will be fought again on other battlefields. But it is quite another thing for an army to study the

171

past, and especially the present, to absorb its lessons, to analyze its successes and failures, to filter out the hard facts that can be applied to a battlefield of the future. For decades following the American Civil War, its decisive battles and campaigns were studied and plotted on the sand tables of such sound military academies as St. Cyr, Sandhurst, and Berlin (even before Civil War operations became a part of the required curriculum at West Point). From those studies emerged grist for the mills that would grind in future wars. *Blitzkrieg* and "total war" seemed novel in the twentieth century, but students of the Civil War knew the concepts as Mahan's credo of surprise, speed, daring, and flexibility and as Sherman's strategy of crushing not only the enemy's army but also the enemy's resources and potential for support of the army. The past anticipated the future; the Civil War anticipated the wars of the century to follow. Similarly, the U.S. Army of tomorrow will be influenced by the successes and failures of yesterday and of today.

In this respect, the war in Viet-Nam has served as a proving ground for the limited war and counterinsurgency tactics and for much of the organizational structure, weaponry, equipment, and doctrine of the U.S. Army in the same way the Spanish Civil War served as a test vehicle for the German Army. The U.S. Army is reluctant to acknowledge this fact because—with good reason—it does not wish to be likened to the German Army of the 1930's and because American involvement in Viet-Nam in no way stems from the availability of that harried country as the ultimate in realistic testing. Nonetheless, no training exercises the Army could possibly devise could ever provide the same knowledge and experience, both in degree and in authenticity. With its dramatic, emphatic affirmation of the helicopter and the airmobile division structure, with its demonstration of the range of tactics of determined, well-supported guerrilla forces, with its exposure of the difficulties of countervailing against a "war of national liberation" while maintaining flexibility to meet conventional and unconventional threats in other arenas, Viet-Nam provides guidelines for charting the Army of the future. Further, the emergence of Red China as a nuclear power and the probability that Peking will have a delivery system sometime in the 1970's underscore the nuclear threat that the Army can never ignore.

In a politico-military context, Viet-Nam emphasizes that the Communist bloc persists in its support of insurgency and guerrilla warfare as major tactics in its long-range strategic objective of dominating the world. Efforts to stimulate uprisings in Laos, Thailand, and elsewhere confirm this intention. There is no reason to expect abandonment of this policy; on the contrary, there is every likelihood that the Communist bloc will adhere to and even expand its support of "wars of national liberation." Nor have the conventional forces of the Communist bloc in Europe remained static. Weaponry, mechanized vehicles, and close air support for the Red Army continue to be upgraded. The Warsaw Pact remains in effect, and although some of its member nations appear to be growing restive within the bonds of the alliance, there is no basis for expecting a dissolution of those bonds. All these factors are determining the direction of the U.S. Army.

One of the most powerful determinants of the future course of the Army is created by science and technology. Deeply involved in a comprehensive research and development program, the Army monitors closely the entire spectrum of scientific activity to obtain forecasts of technological advances that have an application for ground-force exploitation. The latest Army research plan identifies direct ground-force interest in general physics and nuclear physics, chemistry, electronics, energy conversion, mechanics, mathematics, the terrestrial and atmospheric environmental sciences, astronomy and astrophysics, biology, medicine, and the behavioral and social sciences. The Army's objective in all of these scientific fields is to translate laboratory findings into useful equipment, devices, and techniques that help the ground elements to accomplish their mission better, faster, more economically, or more safely. On the basis of the present levels of scientific attainment and the rate at which new knowledge is being converted into practical applications, the Army is able to plan its timetable for technological enhancement of its capabilities and resources.

But it is not enough for the Army to keep abreast of scientific progress in the Free World. It must also be familiar with scientific progress in the Communist bloc in order to prevent the possibility of "technological surprise." To avoid becoming the battlefield victim of enemy technological advances, the Army must know what the enemy has up its scientific sleeve. Thus, the Technical Intelligence Division of the Army Matériel Command is dedicated to unraveling the secrets of the enemy's latest weapons and devices in being and on the drawing boards. This scientific sleuthing is an amalgam of scholarly analysis, technological sophistication, and behind-the-lines probing in the best cloak-and-dagger tradition. By fitting the jigsaw-puzzle pieces together into a mosaic of the enemy's military muscle and his technological potential, the Army is enabled to create defenses and to develop superior countermeasures in advance. From the total scientific effort, both in the Free World and behind the Bamboo and Iron curtains, emerge the characteristics of the ground force "hardware" of the future.

An inescapable aspect of the over-all R&D effort is the future influence of military hardware that the Army has under various stages of development. Weapons, combat vehicles, communications equipment, and all other military matériel, save for a scattering of relatively unsophisticated devices, are long lead-time items. The Army Matériel Command fudges when it calculates four to five years as the average lead-time required for development, production, and procurement of military hardware; this calculation fails to allow for all of the necessary preliminary conceptual and design studies. A more realistic lead-time estimate for sophisticated hardware is eight, nine, and even ten years. This means that on the basis of the matériel undergoing development today, even allowing for the information gaps imposed by the requirements of security, one can judge with reasonable accuracy the characteristics of many of the items that will be going into the Army's inventory in the mid–1970's. Furthermore, because of the predictable lifetime for major items, one can gauge the nature of much of the Army's weaponry and equipment well into the 1980's and, in some cases, to the 1990's.

Another factor shaping the evolving Army is the inescapable pressure of economics. How much money is available to the Army determines how far and how fast it can go in introducing changes. During the Eisenhower era of austere Army budgets, the ground forces were forced to mark time because the money allocations permitted little else. Significantly, although the Army was denied the funds with which to modernize and improve its capabilities, it did not cease planning for improvement in the more affluent days it hoped would come. It was during this period that the Army quietly went about the business of planning the Iroquois and Chinook helicopters and the M-60 machine gun, all of which proved their value when funds finally became available to move them from the drawing boards to reality.

Since 1962, the budget-makers have treated the Army more kindly. This attitude is apt to prevail into the foreseeable future because the threat most actively and most immediately facing the nation is in the ground environment, and this situation will certainly persist for some time to come. But kindliness at the hands of the budget-makers is a relative condition; it does not mean that the Army no longer faces financial stringencies. What it does mean is that in the predictable future the Army can expect to be furnished the funds to introduce improvements if, in fact, they are indeed necessary and are of demonstrable value.

Finally, the Army of the future will be shaped by the total military strategy. At present, the military strategy of multiple options and measured response favors the Army, because the ground forces, to a greater degree than the other services, have the ability to temper their response from a whack across the backside by an MP's billy to the thunder of a tactical atomic missile. There is no way a strategic bomber or a Polaris submarine can whack a backside. Even if it should be necessary to resort to the ultimate madness of a massive nuclear exchange, the Army still has a role to play—two, in fact. Its first mission is to operate the Army's air defense system to blunt the enemy nuclear attack. The second mission is to utilize its versatile talents and resources to rescue the nation from the chaos and awful destruction that all-out nuclear war would bring—and to defend the survivors. Although refinements in the national military strategy can be anticipated, no drastic changes are in sight. Thus, there will continue to be a variety of major roles for the Army to play, and the Army that is evolving is being designed to cope with all of them effectively.

An unexpected technological breakthrough, an international political realignment, a miscalculation or an aberration on the part of the enemy (or by the United States or her allies) can alter the picture completely. But on the premise of what can reasonably be anticipated, taking all known and contemplated factors into consideration, the sort of Army the United States will have in the future can be forecast.

Within its tactical organization, the Army of the foreseeable future will present no radical departures. The ROAD division structure affords commanders the kind of flexibility they have long sought, and there is no reason to suppose that it will be abandoned or even altered to any marked degree. At least one more ROAD airmobile division will be created to join the pioneering 1st Cavalry. The new division will be formed either by conversion of an existing division to the airmobile configuration or by expansion of the present total of Army divisions from seventeen to eighteen—probably the latter. In anticipation of establishment of the new airmobile division, the initial steps have already been taken to procure the long lead-time matériel required to outfit it.

In addition to the new division (or divisions), it is likely that there will be an increase in the number of separate brigades in the Army. A move in this direction was heralded by the action in 1966 to create three new separate brigades. The brigade structure provides an extremely useful unit for rapid deployment to cope with small localized disturbances, to reinforce a division engaged in a larger action, or to serve as an expansible framework that can be enlarged to become a division. The excellent results obtained with the 173d Airborne Brigade (Separate) in the Far East, especially in the fighting in Viet-Nam, demonstrate the validity of the separate brigade as a hard-hitting, self-sufficient, spearhead force. Smaller, lighter, and with logistical requirements greatly reduced from that of a division, the brigade is intended to command and control up to four maneuver battalions.

More than ever before, the Army will become an "all-purpose" force designed for nuclear war, for conventional war, and for limited war. It will be organized and equipped to match weapons and tactics to objectives ranging over the spectrum from complete annihilation of an enemy down to stabilization and containment of an enemy. For operations in the European Theater, which will continue to present a lucrative target for the enemy and, therefore, will continue to pose the most potential danger for the security of the West, the Army will retain a division mix that gives greater emphasis to armor and heavy weapons than the division mix it will maintain in the Far Eastern Theater.

The keystone of the Army's armored force will be a new tank, the Main Battle Tank (MBT), that will be fielded in the early 1970's; it will undoubtedly remain in the active inventory throughout the 1980's. The MBT represents a departure in Army weapons system development procedures, inasmuch as it has been a joint U.S.–German undertaking since the inception of the project. Many of the details of the MBT remain classified, but it is known that the tank, pilot models of which will be ready for testing in 1967–68, will be specifically designed for survival on a nuclear battlefield. It will be heavily armored and highly maneuverable. Its power plant will provide high-speed and long-range capabilities. Its firepower will be built around a versatile, 152-mm. combination gun/launcher capable of firing either Shillelagh surface-to-surface missiles or conventional ammunition. Its fire-control system will incorporate exotic electronic devices that will introduce a new order of accuracy and speed. The MBT will be dimensioned in both metric and inch measurements, and for the interface of major components it will utilize internationally standardized thread-fastener systems; these methods will simplify logistical support and will permit interchangeability of major components in combat.

Although the MBT represents an effort of primary importance and although it will engender in the ground forces a vastly improved armored capability, the Army is not expected to increase its commitment to armored forces to any significant degree. Two interrelated factors mitigate against a quantitative increase in the armored forces. The first factor bearing on the subject is the overwhelming size of the Soviet armored units. With some 55,000 tanks and armored vehicles, the Red Army is by far the most massively armored army in the world; all present indications are that the Russians will continue to accord to tanks a primary role in their military strategy. Because of the mammoth size of the Red Army tank elements, the U.S. Army seeks to avoid being sucked into a tank-for-tank race with the Russians. The cost would be enormous and it would of necessity divert effort from other areas; in the end it would avail nothing except, perhaps, an armored stand-off. The second related factor that makes a quantitative expansion of armor inadvisable is that the Army has a better way to defeat enemy tanks than by depending solely upon a titanic armored confrontation: The Army has developed extremely effective antitank weapons, including heat-seeking missiles that can knock out tanks from airborne flying platforms. The implications of these weapons are readily apparent—moving at a dozen times the ground speed of the tanks and unaffected by the vagaries of the terrain, helicopters or VTOL's can sweep over the battlefield and loose missiles that will home in on the heat of the tank engines. Alternatively, the Army can engage enemy armor with its own tanks or ground antitank weapons. This means that the very massiveness of the Red armored elements can become a liability. It also means that any army that placed primary reliance on vast fleets of armor could find itself in the same straits.

"Fighter" helicopters, more formally labeled "advanced aerial fire support systems" (AAFSS), will be introduced in the Army's inventory in the very early 1970's. Unlike present armed helicopters utilized in Viet-Nam, all of which have had ground-force weaponry hastily added on, these craft will be designed from the very beginning as flying weapons platforms integrating armament specifically created for aerial use. One configuration under expedited development appears to be a likely candidate for adoption as the Army's first operational AAFSS. It will have a rigid rotor system for a high degree of maneuverability and for extreme stability while hovering; it will also have a thrusting pusher-type propeller, short stubby wings, and an antitorque rotor; this combination will permit speeds in level flight at least twice that of the armed helicopters currently employed in Viet-Nam. The aircraft fire-control devices will compute ranges rapidly, track targets automatically, and permit nighttime operation. Weaponry will consist of a mix of antitank missiles, rockets, grenade launchers, and multiple-barrel machine guns. Weapon recoil will be reduced to the vanishing point.

It is probable that Army Aviation will operate at least two different, complementary advanced aerial fire support systems. Unlike the present generation of helicopters, which must be over the enemy in order to engage a target, the AAFSS will be able to deliver "stand-off" fire. Because of its radically improved operational characteristics and weaponry, the AAFSS will assume a variety of missions: fighter escort for troop carriers in airmobile operations, delivery of suppressive fire in landing zones, delivery of area fire against enemy concentrations, and delivery of point target fire against armored vehicles and reinforced enemy emplacements. Highly accurate point target fire will be made possible by a stabilized sight system that will automatically and instantaneously feed course directional change data to the AAFSS's missiles from the time they are launched until the time they impact on target.

The AAFSS is only one of several new craft that Army Aviation will introduce. One, a transitional craft pending final development of the AAFSS concept, is the Huey Cobra, a nearly 200-mile-per-hour armed helicopter scheduled for introduction by 1968. Virtually all of the next generation of Army aircraft will be jet-powered; indeed, this trend is already in evidence. Sometime in the 1970's, VTOL's will certainly join the Army's aircraft inventory. In addition to true vertical take-off and landing craft, the newcomers will include VSTOL's (vertical or short take-off and landing). Both the VTOL's and VSTOL's will conform to the Army's insistence on easy maintainability in the field and on little or no runway requirements. One VSTOL that seems assured of a place in the Army air fleet is the tilt-wing XC-142, now in the experimental stage and showing great promise. Other aircraft in prospect for the future include a "family" of tactical troop carriers with speeds in the 300–500 miles-per-hour range. These will consist of squad-sized carriers for initial assaults, backed by platoon and company-sized carriers for follow-up delivery once the squad has enlarged the airhead sufficiently. For logistical and service-support missions, Army Aviation will maintain high-lift, large-capacity helicopters in various configurations, including detachable pods, sling suspensions, and clamshell-opening fuselages. For some years to come, the huge CH-54 Flying Crane will remain an aerial work horse, while the Army goes ahead with development of an even more effective replacement with a 20-ton lift capacity.

One serious aviation problem that the Army is devoting its resources to solving is "downwash," the high-velocity downdraft created by helicopters and VTOL's on take-off and landing. Downwash, which in the case of jets can attain a velocity of hundreds of miles an hour, sends huge clouds of dust and debris billowing up from the ground, not only obscuring vision but also causing foreign matter to be ingested into jet ports. The Army is seeking a simplified downwash-suppression system, and it seems probable that its search will bear fruit sometime during the 1970's.

Meanwhile, the Army will not be sitting still on the ground. It will continue its efforts to provide better land mobility. Performance on highways has reached such satisfactory levels that it no longer remains a problem; now it is in the area of off-road performance in varying terrain and climatic conditions that the Army will concentrate. As a result, future Army vehicles will be better able to negotiate soft, rough, or steeply pitched terrain, will be more amphibious and more air-transportable, and will be tougher, lighter, faster, more maneuverable, and more easily maintained under combat conditions.

During the 1970's, several new ground vehicles will become operational and will remain standard through the 1980's. They will provide a degree of flexibility and maneuverability that present vehicles cannot approach and that will stem from several innovations and improvements. Power plants will be considerably changed. Engines will not only be more powerful and rugged, but will operate on a variety of fuels in order to end dependence upon a single source. To a very great extent, engines will be interchangeable among various types of vehicles, and the over-all total of different engines employed for land mobility will be reduced. Vehicle hulls will be of unitized construction to increase flotation. Many of the truck bodies will be articulated so that half of the truck can roll, pitch, and yaw in one direction while the other half twists in opposition; yet, all wheels will remain on the ground at all times. Wheeled vehicles will be equipped with over-size, low pressure tires to provide high ground clearance and good traction in mushy going. Likely to make its appearance in the late 1970's is the multi-torque wheel drive; in this system, each individual wheel will include an integral, lightweight, self-contained power plant that will serve either as the main driving system or as an auxiliary when additional traction is desired. Other vehicles under development are ground effects (air cushion) machines; extremely shallow-draft swamp boats powered by aircraft engines; and the Marsh Screw, an amphibious vehicle driven by two spiral-bladed, rotating pontoons that propel it over sand, water, snow, mud, paddies, or marsh.

Probably the first of the new-generation vehicles to become operational will be a 5-ton truck to replace both the existing 5-ton and 2½-ton trucks. It will be driven by a 210-horsepower, multifuel engine and will be equipped with automatic transmission, power steering, and power brakes. Its primary function will be as a troop and cargo carrier and as a tow for the 155-mm. howitzer. Adapted with a special body, it will serve as a tanker, a wrecker, or a dump truck. It will be amphibious and air-droppable and will weigh about 2 tons less than the present 5-ton truck. If this truck is beaten out as the first of the new vehicles to become operational, it will most likely be by the XM-561, an articulated, 6-wheel drive truck. Highly versatile, it will be employed in numerous roles including firing platform, ambulance, command post, communications center, and weapons carrier. Completely floatable, it will attain a water speed of about 2 miles per hour using only the rotation of its wheels for propulsion.

A new vehicular concept, the mechanized infantry combat vehicle, is expected to be fielded by 1975. A squad carrier, it will feature a large rear ramp to permit infantrymen to embark and disembark rapidly. It will be fully armored and fully tracked. A cupola on the top of the hull will mount a 20-mm. automatic gun and a 7.62-mm. coaxial light machine gun. It will probably utilize the same 425-horsepower engine, transmission, and suspension system that have been so successful on the M-107/M-110 group of self-propelled artillery. It will have a top speed of about 40 miles per hour and a range of 400 miles.

It is possible that a family of radical, combat support vehicles will appear in the Army's inventory in the 1980's. Among the initial concepts being bandied about in Army R&D laboratories are a tracked, armored, earth-tunneling machine mounting a high-speed, high-capacity, universally jointed boring screw; a gigantic self-propelled shoreline barrier breacher that would cut passages for amphibious landings through rock up to 40 feet high; and a full-tracked, multiarmed rubble remover to clear 12-foot passages through destroyed areas.

The weapons that the Army will employ in the future will be more rugged, more versatile, more easily maintained, and more accurate. Fire-control devices will be more sophisticated, yet at the same time less complicated to operate, and they will have a much greater all-weather capability. Sensing systems incorporating advanced infrared, accoustical, radar, and, eventually, laser devices, will permit highly effective nighttime target acquisition and identification. Among several weapons under development for the 1970's are improved mortars, cannon with higher velocities and more rapid rates of fire, a machine gun/rocket launcher combination, and a new rifle—the SPIW—to give the soldier a single weapon with the dispersed fire effect of a grenade launcher and the pinpoint fire of a rifle. The SPIW could be in the hands of the troops as early as 1970–71.

A very significant tactical weapon that is expected to be deployed around 1968 is the TOW (tube-launched, optically automatically tracked, wire-guided) antitank system. The TOW will be capable of defeating any known tank currently in operation or foreseen up to the 1980 time-frame. Highly mobile, the TOW will fire a missile with a conventional warhead. It will give the infantry its first automatic antitank system wherein the gunner has merely to keep his sight fixed on the target and the missile will be automatically directed toward the kill. Even more dramatic antitank weapons are in store further in the future. One concept under study is a missile with a guidance brain that can find the target and home the missile in on it. The Army is learning how to program into such a missile's guidance system an electronic picture of how a tank will appear in relation to its natural surroundings. Once all of the enormously complicated problems are solved, the launch crew will simply program into the guidance system a map of the situation ahead, will launch the missile, and then will leave it to the missile itself to find an enemy tank and knock it out. Such an amazing antitank weapons system could become operational by the 1990's.

An across-the-board objective of the Army is to strive for multipurpose battlefield missiles to the greatest extent possible. In essence, the aim is to make one missile system do the jobs that it now takes several to accomplish—for instance, to develop a single system that can engage a moving target, a static target, or a reinforced target. The Army is also seeking to build a twofold capacity into its long-range, tactical missiles. These missiles reach out far beyond the range of conventional artillery, but at present are equipped solely with nuclear warheads—which means that they can be used for a nuclear strike or not at all. The aim is to build in additional capability for a conventional response at a range many times in excess of the normal reach of artillery.

By the early 1970's, Lance, a highly mobile surface-to-surface tactical missile in the 20–25-mile range, will be operational as a replacement for the aging Honest John and the Lacrosse; it may also supersede Little John, although this is not a certainty. Lance will be the first Army missile to use prepackaged, storable, liquid propellant. For tactical air defense on the battlefield, the Army will introduce SAM-D, a mobile and rugged missile that will be the principal tactical air defense system throughout the 1970's and into the 1980's. Future missiles now in early stages of development will attain radically high velocities imparted by new, very-high-burn-rate propellants; refinements in airframe and structural engineering will enable the missiles to sustain the terrific velocities they will achieve.

The Army is in a paradoxical position concerning strategic air defense within the continental United States. It depends for this on the Nike-Hercules and Hawk missiles, both of which are effective against aircraft but neither of which has an antimissile kill capability. The paradox comes from the fact that the Army has made excellent progress in development of two first-rate anti-ICBM missiles in its Nike-X program, but whether or not it will ever reach the point of procurement and deployment is a moot question. The matter depends upon decisions and funding action by the Secretary of Defense, Congress, and the President. In the meantime, the Army can only proceed with development of the missiles and their associated target detection, identification, discrimination, tracking, and other systems at the pace and to the extent that it is permitted to do so.

The two Nike-X missiles are the Sprint and the Spartan, a redesigned version of the Zeus. Sprint, a 27-foot, spike-nosed, solid-propellent weapon, accelerates with such incredible speed that the computers that plot its course to intercept an incoming missile must function in nanoseconds (one-billionth of a second). Development of Sprint is well advanced; initial test firing of a prototype in 1965 was very successful. The second Nike-X missile, Spartan, a three-stage, solid-propellent, long-range interceptor, does not accelerate as rapidly as Sprint, but has a much longer reach. It is intended for the distant interception and destruction of ICBM's or hostile orbiting satellites. Early Zeus missiles have already proved themselves by the actual interception of ICBM test targets and by the simulated interception of a satellite in orbit. Both Spartan and Sprint are planned as complementary missiles—Sprint to race at amazing speed to destroy any enemy targets that succeed in evading the long reach of Spartan. If it were given a go-ahead and the funds required to do the job, the Army could have the Nike-X system in place in the United States in the 1970's.

The emerging Army will be supported by an array of highly developed electronic devices that will be fast, light, small, and versatile. By 1969, troop units should be using very efficient solid-state communications switchboards. Throughout the 1970's and the 1980's, the present generation of miniaturized communications devices will give way to microminiature successors that will be dramatically smaller. An indication of things to come is the Army's development in 1966 of a radio-wave signal generator that is the size of a grain of rice. Despite its exceedingly diminutive size, it has almost unprecedented signal-strength output in relation to electric-power input. Furthermore, the signal generator is very durable and is compatible with the microminiature circuitry under development for a number of electronic applications.

Automatic data processing will become a common technique of widespread utilization in the field in the future Army. By the early 1970's, tactical automatic data-processing equipment will be in routine use down to division level for such applications as intelligence, fire support, logistics, and administration. Smaller, simpler, cheaper ADP equipment will be utilized at battalion level for fire control and stock control. ADP will be no substitute for human judgment; its great contribution will come from its instant retrieval of vital data from among the mountains of information stored in its electronic memory.

The rapid advances in electronics will leave an unmistakable mark on the Army's capability in battlefield surveillance and target acquisition. Well along in development is the MQM-58A, an airborne surveillance system built around an unmanned aircraft and associated electronic equipment. The MQM-58A will permit high-speed reconnaissance flights in daylight or darkness; it could be in operation as early as 1969–70. A more sophisticated system under study utilizes a high-performance aerial vehicle, advanced sensors, automatic data-processing links, and electronic devices; it could be deployed in the mid-1970's

The U.S. Army that takes to the field in the next quarter-century will be enormously altered in virtually every aspect of its matériel. The new equipment, devices, weapons, and vehicles highlighted above are only the peaks of the iceberg. A random sampling of some of the many other items on the way includes remotely steered cargo-delivery parachutes; supersensitive mine detectors, including an airborne model that will skim ahead of advancing troops to clear the route; and a demolition explosive that looks like a giant band-aid, and is tough, flexible, insensitive to shock and weather extremes, can be cut in pieces, and will stick to anything when its adhesive backing is peeled away. The changes in matériel, its greater variety and sophistication, will aggravate the Army's logistical burden. To make matters worse, the vastly augmented firepower and horsepower of the Army will make for an enormous step-up in resupply requirements. This trend has already made itself felt. Today in Viet-Nam, for instance, the average ROAD division uses two or three times the resupply tonnage that was needed by a division as recently as the Korean War. To maintain operational mobility, the 1st Cavalry Division (Airmobile) must be supplied with a daily average of 350 short tons of aviation gas alone. All of these quantitative needs will continue to grow.

To prevent logistics from strangling the ground forces, the Army is going ahead full speed on a number of logistics-related projects in addition to automatic data-processing, better and faster delivery systems, greater durability and easier maintenance of the entire range of matériel, multifuel vehicle engines, and multipurpose weapons. One of the most outstanding R&D projects is development of a practical fuel cell to convert hydrogen and air directly into electrical energy. These silent electric-generation devices will, when perfected, have a much more favorable weight-to-energy-output ratio than conventional engines and will have reduced fuel requirements. Fuel cells with a generation capacity up to 15,000 watts will be ready for field-testing in the 1968–70 period.

It is very possible that by 1975 several of the Army's communications and surveillance devices will be powered by fuel cells. A short time later, portable fuel cells that will generate electrical power for missile complexes should follow. Perhaps around 1980, the Army will field the first fuel-cell-powered light trucks. These will be dual-purpose vehicles. Like any other standard truck, they will serve as troop and cargo carriers. However, when stationary and with engines idling, they will serve as generators of electricity for external use.

Possibly the most "Buck Rogerish" of all Army R&D concepts is a device to counteract the pull of the earth's gravitational system. Despite its seeming to be a pursuit better left to the writers of science fiction, the Army is quite serious in its search for a successful antigravity technique. It would be a mistake to dismiss this effort too lightly, especially in view of the Army's demonstrated ability to bring to fruition techniques and devices that were within the realm of science fiction only a generation or two ago. The implications of an eventual breakthrough in the endeavor to overcome gravity are tremendous. One immediate result would be its impact on logistics. A major portion of the fuel used by a vehicle is expended in simply counteracting gravitational force. If a means could be found to neutralize gravity, the Army's fuel requirements would be sharply curtailed.

But antigravity devices lie in the distant future. Predictable for the next twenty years or so is that the Army will field a ground force as different in its weaponry, vehicles, equipment and matériel as today's Army is different from the one that faced the enemy in 1941.

The Army is more than military hardware. It is people. More than ever, the Army will consider its most valuable single resource and its most potent individual weapon to be the soldier. Tomorrow's soldier will be, on average, younger, better educated, more highly trained, and more at home amid the growing sophistication of ground-force matériel. The massive efforts of the civilian community to upgrade education will be reflected in the recruits. Attractive early-retirement policies of the military will return the soldier to civilian life at a relatively young age. Increased emphasis on early promotion to high rank will keep the officer corps youthful. When they "fade away" in the future, "old soldiers" will not be so old as they once were.

More widespread utilization of closed-circuit television and of electronic teaching machines will improve training, making it more standardized, more intensive, and more effective. Field training will become flexible as it is altered to absorb the lessons learned from the combat in Viet-Nam. Already planned for incorporation into field training as a result of experience in Viet-Nam is added emphasis on night maneuvers, on tactical operations in populated areas, and on riot control. Training in foreign languages will become more common, particularly for officers and noncommissioned officers.

The personal equipment of tomorrow's soldiers will give them enhanced protection in combat. Improved, lighter body armor is in the terminal stages of development. Particular attention has been paid to headgear, and a new, considerably safer flight helmet will soon be issued to Army aviators. Before 1970, ground elements should have a new nylon helmet that will provide significantly greater protection against small-arms fire and shrapnel. By the mid-1970's, for the first time, soldiers will have available eye armor that will reduce battle injury to eyes by more than 50 per cent. The Army is also working on goggles that will protect against intense light; the lenses will darken instantly in the presence of strong sunlight or the flash that accompanies an explosive burst and then will automatically resume complete transparency when the intensity of the light has returned to normal levels. The uniforms of the future will provide improved protection againt chemical attack and against climatic extremes.

Medical care for the soldier will reach new heights of effectiveness, and the combat mortality rate will reach an irreducible minimum. Periods of hospitalization will become progressively shorter. These circumstances will result from several factors. Preventive medicine, including longer-lasting and more effective vaccines, will give the soldier stronger defenses against the invisible tyrant of the battlefield—disease. More rapid, more efficacious surgical techniques and devices will assure swifter, more complete recovery from combat wounds. Evacuation from the battlefield to stabilized hospital complexes will be faster, thanks to better mobility, but it will not be necessary as frequently because combat medical techniques will be better. Many medical procedures that now have to be performed in rear areas will, in the future, be performed at the front. Indicative of this trend toward moving medical resources forward are two new developments: a light-weight, fully portable, very rugged X-ray unit, which has been tested successfully on the battlefield in Viet-Nam, and a field autoclave, or sterilizer, that uses any external heat source and is specifically designed for use in isolated areas common to guerrilla warfare situations.

The U.S. Army today is the finest the nation has ever produced. It is alert, vigorous, imaginative, and professional. It is admirably armed and equipped. It is well organized, and its tactical concepts are eminently sound. Perhaps most significant, it is a dynamic force. The resistance to change that at various times in the past has hampered the Army has been abandoned. Today's Army welcomes change and is dedicating its energies and its resources to the successful support of the national strategy of today and tomorrow.

Eventually, all strategies revolve around the fundamental, immutable truth that as long as man's political, economic, and social institutions are rooted in the ground, it is in the ground environment that they must ultimately be defended. Wherever wars may commence, it is on the land that they must end. Consequently, as long as the nation must bear arms as a guarantee of its security, it must look to the Army as the ultimate guarantor. The Army of the United States has never been more capable of carrying that burden.

APPENDIX I

The Regular Army Divisions

Name	Nickname	Location (1967)
1st Armored Division	Old Ironsides	Fort Hood, Texas
1st Infantry Division	The Big Red One	Viet-Nam
1st Cavalry Division (Airmobile)	The First Team	Viet-Nam
2d Armored Division	Hell on Wheels	Fort Hood, Texas
2d Infantry Division	Indianhead	Korea
3d Armored Division	Spearhead Division	Germany
3d Infantry Division (Mechanized)	The Marne Division	Germany
4th Armored Division		Germany
4th Infantry Division	Ivy Division	Viet-Nam
5th Infantry Division (Mechanized)	Red Diamond	Fort Carson, Colorado
7th Infantry Division	Bayonet Division	Korea
8th Infantry Division (Mechanized)	Golden Arrow	Germany
9th Infantry Division	Old Reliables	Viet-Nam
24th Infantry Division	Victory Division	Germany
25th Infantry Division	Tropic Lightning	Viet-Nam
82d Airborne Division	All American	Fort Bragg, North Carolina
101st Airborne Division	Screaming Eagles	Fort Campbell, Kentucky, and Viet-Nam

APPENDIX II

U.S. Army Areas

Designation	States or Other Territory Included	Headquarters
Military District of Washington (MDW)	District of Columbia; Arlington, Fairfax, King George, Prince William, Stafford, and Westmoreland counties, and the city of Alexandria, Va.; and Calvert, Charles, Montgomery, Prince Georges, and St. Mary's counties, Md.	Room 1619, Tempo B, 2d and R Sts., S. W., Washington, D.C. 20315
First U.S. Army	Conn., Del., Ky., Md. (less area allocated to MDW), Mass., N.H., N.J., N.Y., Ohio, Pa., R.I., Vt., Va. (less area allocated to MDW), and W.Va.	Ft. George G. Meade, Md. 20755
Third U.S. Army	Ala., Fla., Ga., Miss., N.C., S.C., and Tenn.	Ft. McPherson, Ga. 30330
Fourth U.S. Army	Ark., La., N.Mex., Okla., and Texas	Ft. Sam Houston, Texas 78234
Fifth U.S. Army	Colo., Ind., Ill., Iowa, Kan., Mich., Minn., Mo., Neb., N.D., S.D., Wis., and Wyo.	1660 E. Hyde Park Blvd., Chicago, Ill. 60615
Sixth U.S. Army	Ariz., Calif., Idaho, Mont., Nev., Utah, Ore., and Wash.	Presidio of San Francisco, San Francisco, Calif. 94129

APPENDIX III

Active Army Installations and Major Activities in the Continental United States (by Army Area)

Installation or Activity	Location	Post Office Address
Military District of Washington		
Arlington Hall Station	4000 Arlington Blvd. Arlington, Va. 22212	Same
Army Map Service	6500 Brooks Lane, N.W. Washington, D.C. 20315	Same
Belvoir, Fort	Accotink, Va.	Fort Belvoir, Va. 22060
Cameron Station	Alexandria, Va. 22314	Same
Harry Diamond Laboratories	Connecticut Ave. & Van Ness St., N.W. Washington, D.C. 20438	Same
McNair, Fort Lesley J.	4th & P Sts., S.W. Washington, D.C. 20315	Same
Myer, Fort	Arlington, Va.	Fort Myer, Va. 22208
Vint Hills Farms Station	Warrenton, Va. 22186	Same
Walter Reed Army Medical Center	6925 16th St., N.W. Washington, D.C.	Washington, D.C. 20012
First U.S. Army Area		
Aberdeen Proving Ground	Aberdeen, Md.	Aberdeen Proving Ground, Md. 21005
Army Pictorial Center	35–11 35th Ave. Long Island City, N.Y. 11101	Same
Banks, Fort	Winthrop, Mass. 02152	Same
Blue Grass Depot Activity	Fort Estill, Ky.	Richmond, Ky. 40475
Boston Army Base	666 Summer St. Boston, Mass. 02110	Same
Brooklyn Army Terminal	1st Ave. & 58th St. Brooklyn, N.Y. 11250	Same

193

Installation or Activity	Location	Post Office Address
Carlisle Barracks	Carlisle, Pa.	Carlisle Barracks, Pa. 17013
Cleveland Army Tank–Automotive Plant	6200 Riverside Dr. Cleveland, Ohio 44125	Same
Columbus Army Depot	East Broad Street Columbus, Ohio	Columbus, Ohio 43215
Detrick, Fort	Frederick, Md. 21701	Same
Devens, Fort	Ayer, Mass.	Fort Devens, Mass. 01433
Dix, Fort	Wrightstown, N.J.	Fort Dix, N.J. 08640
Edgewood Arsenal	Edgewood Arsenal, Md. 21040	Same
Erie Army Depot	Port Clinton, Ohio, 43452	Same
Eustis, Fort	Lee Hall, Va.	Fort Eustis, Va. 32604
Frankford Arsenal	Bridge & Tacony Sts. Philadelphia, Pa. 19137	Same
Hamilton, Fort	Brooklyn, N.Y.	Fort Hamilton, N.Y. 11209
Hampton Roads Army Terminal	7737 Hampton Blvd. Norfolk, Va. 23505	Same
Hancock, Fort	Highlands, N.J. 07732	Same
Holabird, Fort	Baltimore, Md.	Fort Holabird, Md. 20219
Jay, Fort	Governors Island New York, N.Y. 10004	Same
Knox, Fort	Fort Knox, Ky. 40120	Same
Lee, Fort	Petersburg, Va.	Fort Lee, Va. 23801
Letterkenny Army Depot	Culbertson, Pa.	Chambersburg, Pa. 17201
Lexington Army Depot	Avon, Ky.	Lexington, Ky. 40501
Meade, Fort George G.	Odenton, Md.	Fort George G. Meade, Md. 20755

Installation or Activity	Location	Post Office Address
Miller Field	New Dorp, Staten Island, N.Y.	Fort Wadsworth, Staten Island, N.Y. 10301
Monmouth, Fort	Oceanport, N.J.	Fort Monmouth, N.J. 07703
Monroe, Fort	Old Point Comfort, Va.	Fort Monroe, Va. 23351
Natick Laboratories	Kansas St. Natick, Mass. 01760	Same
New Cumberland Army Depot	New Cumberland, Pa. 17070	Same
Philadelphia Quartermaster Center, U.S. Army	2800 S. 20th St. Philadelphia, Pa. 19145	Same
Picatinny Arsenal	Picatinny, N.J.	Dover, N.J. 07801
Radford Army Ammunition Plant	Pepper, Va.	Radford, Va. 24141
Richmond Quartermaster Depot	Richmond, Va. 23212	Same
Ritchie, Fort	Cascade, Md.	Fort Ritchie, Md. 21719
Rodman, Fort	New Bedford, Mass. 02740	Same
Schenectady Army Depot	Schenectady, N.Y. 12301	Same
Scranton Army Ammunition Plant	156 Cedar Ave. Scranton, Pa. 18502	Same
Seneca Army Depot	Romulus, N.Y. 14541	Same
Slocum, Fort	New Rochelle, N.Y.	Fort Slocum, N.Y. 10801
Springfield Armory	Springfield, Mass. 01101	Same
Story, Fort	Virginia Beach, Va.	Fort Story, Va. 23459
Tilden, Fort	Rockaway Park, Long Island, N.Y.	Fort Tilden, N.Y. 11695

Installation or Activity	Location	Post Office Address
Tobyhanna Army Depot	Tobyhanna, Pa., 18466	Same
Totten, Fort	Bayside, Long Island, N.Y.	Fort Totten, N.Y. 11359
United States Military Academy	West Point, N.Y. 10996	Same
Valley Forge General Hospital	Phoenixville, Pa., 19460	Same
Wadsworth, Fort	Rosebank, Staten Island, N.Y. 10303	Same
Watertown Arsenal	Watertown, Mass. 02172	Same
Watervliet Arsenal	Watervliet, N.Y. 12189	Same
West Point Military Reservation	West Point, N.Y. 10996	Same
	Third U.S. Army Area	
Anniston Army Depot	Bynum, Ala.	Anniston, Ala. 36200
Atlanta Army Depot	Forest Park, Ga. 30050	Same
Benning, Fort	Columbus, Ga.	Fort Benning, Ga. 31905
Bragg, Fort	Fayetteville, N.C.	Fort Bragg, N.C. 28307
Campbell, Fort	Clarksville, Tenn.	Fort Campbell, Ky. 42223
Charleston Army Depot	North Charleston, S.C. 29406	Same
Charlotte Army Missile Plant	1820 Statesville Ave. Charlotte, N.C. 28206	Same
Gordon, Fort	Grovetown, Ga.	Fort Gordon, Ga. 30905
Holston Army Ammunition Plant	Holston, Tenn.	Kingsport, Tenn. 37660
Jackson, Fort	Columbia, S.C.	Fort Jackson, S.C. 29207
McClellan, Fort	Anniston, Ala.	Fort McClellan, Ala. 36205

Installation or Activity	Location	Post Office Address
McPherson, Fort	Atlanta, Ga.	Fort McPherson, Ga. 30330
Memphis Army Depot	Memphis, Tenn. 38115	Same
Milan Army Ammunition Plant	Milan, Tenn. 38358	Same
Phosphate Development Works	Muscle Shoals, Ala. 35662	Same
Redstone Arsenal	Redstone Arsenal, Ala. 35808	Same
Rucker, Fort	Daleville, Ala.	Fort Rucker, Ala. 36362
Stewart, Fort	Hinesville, Ga.	Fort Stewart, Ga. 31314
Sunny Point Army Terminal	Southport, N.C. 28461	Same
Tarheel Army Missile Plant	Burlington, N.C. 27215	Same

Fourth U.S. Army Area

Beaumont, William, General Hospital	Fort Bliss, Texas	William Beaumont General Hospital, Texas 79920
Bliss, Fort	El Paso, Texas	Fort Bliss, Texas 79906
Brooke Army Medical Center	Fort Sam Houston, Texas 78234	Same
Chaffee, Fort	Fort Smith, Ark.	Fort Chaffee, Ark. 72905
Fort Worth Army Depot	Fort Worth, Texas	PO Box 6988 Fort Worth, Texas 76115
Hood, Fort	Killeen, Texas	Fort Hood, Texas 76545
Houston, Fort Sam	San Antonio, Texas	Fort Sam Houston, Texas 78234

Installation or Activity	Location	Post Office Address
Longhorn Army Ammunition Plant	Karnack, Texas	Marshall, Texas 75671
Louisiana Army Ammunition Plant	Doyline, La.	Shreveport, La. 71102
New Orleans Army Terminal	Poland & Dauphine Sts. New Orleans, La. 70140	Same
Pine Bluff Arsenal	Pine Bluff, Ark.	Arsenal, Ark. 71603
Polk, Fort	Leesville, La.	Fort Polk, La. 71446
Red River Army Depot	Hooks, Texas	Texarkana, Texas 75500
Sandia Base	Albuquerque, N.Mex.	Sandia Base, N.Mex. 87115
Sill, Fort	Lawton, Okla.	Fort Sill, Okla. 73504
Stanley, Camp, Storage Activity	San Antonio, Texas 78206	Same
White Sands Missile Range	Las Cruces, N.Mex.	White Sands Missile Range, N.Mex. 88002
Wingate Army Depot, Fort	Gallup, N.Mex. 87301	Same
Wolters, Fort	Mineral Wells, Texas 76067	Same
Fifth U.S. Army Area		
Black Hills Army Depot	Igloo, S.Dak. 57749	Same
Carson, Fort	Colorado Springs, Colo.	Fort Carson, Colo. 80913
Detroit Arsenal	Warren, Mich. 48090	Same
Elwood Ordnance Plant	Elwood, Ill.	Joliet, Ill. 60431
Fitzsimmons General Hospital	Denver, Colo. 80240	Same
Granite City Army Depot	Granite City, Ill. 62040	Same

Installation or Activity	Location	Post Office Address
Hale, Camp	Pando, Colo.	Leadville, Colo. 80461
Harrison, Fort Benjamin	Indianapolis, Ind.	Fort Benjamin Harrison, Ind. 46216
Indiana Army Ammunition Plant	Charlestown, Ind. 47111	Same
Iowa Army Ammunition Plant	Burlington, Iowa 52600	Same
Lake City Army Ammunition Plant	Lake City, Mo.	Independence, Mo. 64050
Leavenworth, Fort	Leavenworth, Kan.	Fort Leavenworth, Kan. 66027
Michigan Army Missile Plant	Warren, Mich. 48090	Same
Muskegon Army Engine Plant	Muskegon, Mich. 49440	Same
Newport Army Ammunition Plant	Newport, Ind. 47966	Same
Pueblo Army Depot	Avondale, Colo.	Pueblo, Colo. 81001
Riley, Fort	Junction City, Kan.	Fort Riley, Kan. 66442
Rock Island Arsenal	Rock Island, Ill. 61200	Same
Rocky Mountain Arsenal	Denver, Colo. 80240	Same
Savanna Army Depot	Savanna, Ill. 61074	Same
Sheridan, Fort	Highwood, Ill.	Fort Sheridan, Ill. 60037
Sioux Army Depot	Sidney, Neb. 69162	Same
U.S. Army Support Center, Chicago	1660 E. Hyde Park Blvd. Chicago, Ill. 60615	Same
Wayne, Fort	6301 W. Jefferson Ave. Detroit, Mich. 48217	Same

Installation or Activity	Location	Post Office Address
Wood, Fort Leonard	Waynesville, Mo.	Fort Leonard Wood, Mo. 65475
	Sixth U.S. Army Area	
Baker, Fort	San Francisco, Calif.	Fort Baker, Calif. 94965
Barry, Fort	San Francisco, Calif.	Sausalito, Calif. 94965
Beaver Army Terminal	Clatskanie, Ore. 97016	Same
Cronkhite, Fort	San Francisco, Calif.	Sausalito, Calif. 94965
Desert Rock, Camp	Indian Springs, Nev.	Las Vegas, Nev. 89101
Douglas, Fort	Salt Lake City, Utah	Fort Douglas, Utah 84113
Dugway Proving Ground	Dugway, Utah 84022	Same
Huachuca, Fort	Fort Huachuca, Ariz. 85613	Same
Hunter Liggett Military Reservation	Jolon, Calif. 93928	Same
Irwin, Fort	Barstow, Calif.	Fort Irwin, Calif. 92311
Lawton, Fort	Seattle, Wash.	Fort Lawton, Wash. 98199
Letterman General Hospital	Presidio of San Francisco, Calif. 94129	Same
Lewis, Fort	Tacoma, Wash.	Fort Lewis, Wash. 98433
MacArthur, Fort	San Pedro, Calif.	Fort MacArthur, Calif. 90733
Madigan General Hospital	Fort Lewis, Wash.	Tacoma, Wash. 98431
Mason, Fort	Bay & Van Ness Ave. San Francisco, Calif.	Fort Mason, Calif. 94129

Installation or Activity	Location	Post Office Address
Monterey, Presidio of	Monterey, Calif.	Presidio of Monterey, Calif. 93940
Navajo Army Depot	Bellemont, Ariz.	Flagstaff, Ariz. 86000
Oakland Army Terminal	Oakland, Calif. 94614	Same
Ord, Fort	Monterey, Calif.	Fort Ord, Calif. 93941
Pasadena Area Support Center	95 S. Grand Ave. Pasadena, Calif. 91105	Same
Sacramento Army Depot	Sacramento, Calif. 95814	Same
San Francisco, Presidio of	San Francisco, Calif.	Presidio of San Francisco, Calif. 94129
Scott, Fort Winfield	San Francisco, Calif.	Presidio of San Francisco, Calif. 94129
Sharpe Army Depot	Lathrop, Calif. 95330	Same
Sierra Army Depot	Herlong, Calif. 96113	Same
Tooele Army Depot	Tooele, Utah 84074	Same
Two Rock Ranch Station	Petaluma, Calif. 94952	Same
Umatilla Army Depot	Hermiston, Ore. 97838	Same
Utah Army Depot	Ogden, Utah 84402	Same
Yakima Firing Center	Yakima, Wash. 98901	Same
Yuma Proving Ground	Yuma, Ariz. 85364	Same

Bibliography

The publications listed below will prove helpful to any readers wishing to accompany the U.S. Army further on its long march. Some of the works are milestones in military literature. Others give lucid explanations of specialized aspects of the Army or bring into focus the Army's personality and atmosphere.

Official Works

Department of the Army. *The United States Army in World War II.* Washington, D.C.: Government Printing Office. This multivolume series, begun in 1947, is not yet completed. Especially recommended are: *The Organization of Ground Combat Troops,* 1947; *Washington Command Post: The Operations Division,* 1951; *Cross Channel Attack,* 1951; *Logistical Support of the Armies, Vol. I,* 1953; *The Organization and Role of the Army Service Forces,* 1954; and *Command Decisions,* 1960.

———. *Dictionary of United States Army Terms.* Washington, D.C.: Department of the Army, 1965.

Joint Chiefs of Staff. *Dictionary of United States Military Terms for Joint Usage.* Washington, D.C.: Department of Defense, 1962.

McNamara, Robert S. *Statement of Secretary of Defense Robert S. McNamara Before The Senate Subcommittee on Department of Defense Appropriations on the Fiscal Year 1967–71 Defense Program and 1967 Defense Budget.* Washington, D.C.: Department of Defense, 1966.

Upton, Major General Emory. *Military Policy of the United States.* 4th Impression. Washington, D. C.: Government Printing Office, 1917.

Books

ARON, RAYMOND. *On War.* New York: Doubleday & Co., 1959.

BACON, ROBERT, and SCOTT, JAMES B. (eds.). *The Military and Colonial Policy of The United States; Addresses and Reports by Elihu Root.* Cambridge, Mass.: Harvard University Press, 1916.

BERNARDO, C. JOSEPH, and BACON, E. H. *American Military Policy.* Harrisburg, Pa.: Military Service Publishing Company, 1955.

BRODIE, BERNARD. *Strategy in the Missile Age.* Princeton, N.J.: Princeton University Press, 1959.

DEITCHMAN, SEYMOUR J. *Limited War and American Defense Policy.* Cambridge, Mass.: M.I.T. Press, 1964.

DUPUY, R. ERNEST, and DUPUY, TREVOR N. *Military Heritage of America.* New York: McGraw-Hill, 1956.

GALULA, DAVID. *Counterinsurgency Warfare: Theory and Practice.* New York: Frederick A. Praeger, 1964.

GANDE, WILLIAM A. *History of the United States Army.* New York: Appleton-Century-Crofts, 1942.

GARTHOFF, RAYMOND L. *The Soviet Image of Future War.* Washington, D.C.: Public Affairs Press, 1959.

GAVIN, JAMES M. *War and Peace in the Space Age.* New York: Harper & Bros., 1958.

GREENFIELD, KENT R. (ed.). *Command Decisions.* New York: Harcourt, Brace, 1960.

HAHN, WALTER F., and NEFF, JOHN C. (eds.). *American Strategy for the Nuclear Age.* New York: Doubleday & Co., 1960.

HITCH, CHARLES J., and McKEAN, ROLAND N. *The Economics of Defense in the Nuclear Age.* Cambridge, Mass.: Harvard University Press, 1960.

HOROWITZ, ROBERT S., *et al. The Ramparts We Watch.* Derby, Conn.: Monarch, 1964.

JACOBS, JAMES RIPLEY. *The Beginning of the U.S. Army.* Princeton, N.J.: Princeton University Press, 1947.

JANOWITZ, MORRIS. *The Professional Soldier.* New York: The Free Press of Glencoe, 1964.

KAHN, HERMAN. *On Thermonuclear War.* Princeton, N.J.: Princeton University Press, 1961.

KAUFMANN, WILLIAM W. *The McNamara Strategy.* New York: Harper & Row, 1964.

KINTNER, WILLIAM R., et al. *Forging a New Sword*. New York: Harper & Bros., 1958.

KNORR, KLAUS E. (ed.). *NATO and American Security*. Princeton, N.J.: Princeton University Press, 1959.

LIDDELL HART, B. H. *Deterrent or Defense: A Fresh Look at the West's Military Position*. New York: Frederick A. Praeger, 1960.

―――. *Strategy*. New York: Frederick A. Praeger, 1954.

MARSHALL, S. L. A. *Men Against Fire*. New York: William Morrow, 1947.

―――. *The River and the Gauntlet*. New York: William Morrow, 1953.

MEDARIS, JOHN B. *Countdown for Decision*. New York: Putnam, 1960.

MILLIS, WALTER, et al. *Arms and the State: Civil-Military Elements in National Policy*. New York: Twentieth Century Fund, 1958.

NICHOLAS, JACK D. et al. *The Joint and Combined Staff Officer's Manual*. Harrisburg, Pa.: The Stackpole Co., 1959.

OSANKA, FRANKLIN M. (ed.). *Modern Guerrilla Warfare: Fighting Communist Guerrilla Movements, 1941–1961*. New York: The Free Press of Glencoe, 1962.

PARSON, NELS A. *Missiles and the Revolution in Warfare*. Cambridge, Mass.: Harvard University Press, 1962.

RAYMOND, JACK. *Power at the Pentagon*. New York: Harper & Row, 1964.

REINHARDT, G. C., and KINTNER, W. R. *Atomic Weapons in Land Combat*. Harrisburg, Pa.: Military Service Publishing Co., 1953.

REYNOLDS, RUSSEL B. *The Officer's Guide*. Harrisburg, Pa.: The Stackpole Co., 1966.

SIGAUD, LOUIS A. *Air Power and Unification*. Harrisburg, Pa.: Military Service Publishing Co., 1949.

―――. *Douhet and Aerial Warfare*. New York: Putnam, 1941.

SOKOLOVSKY, V. D. *Military Strategy*. New York: Frederick A. Praeger, 1963.

SPAULDING, OLIVER L. *The United States Army in War and Peace*. New York: Putnam, 1937.

STRAUSZ-HUPÉ, ROBERT, et al. *A Forward Strategy for America*. New York: Harper & Bros., 1961.

―――. *Protracted Conflict*. New York: Harper & Bros., 1959.

TAYLOR, MAXWELL D. *The Uncertain Trumpet*. New York: Harper & Bros., 1960.

THAYER, CHARLES W. *Guerrilla*. New York: Harper & Row, 1963.

TODD, FREDERICK P., and KREDEL, FRITZ. *Soldiers of the American Army—1775–1954*. Chicago, Ill.: Henry Regnery, 1954.

WEIGLEY, RUSSELL F. *Towards an American Army*. New York: Columbia University Press, 1962.

WOLFERS, ARNOLD (ed.). *Alliance Policy in the Cold War*. Baltimore, Md.: Johns Hopkins Press, 1959.

YOUNG, GORDON R. (ed.). *The Army Almanac*. Harrisburg, Pa.: The Stackpole Co., 1959.

Periodicals

Armor, The Magazine of Mobile Warfare. Washington, D.C.: United States Armor Association.

Army. Washington, D.C.: Association of the United States Army.

Army Digest. Washington, D.C.: Department of the Army.

Infantry Magazine. Fort Benning, Ga.: The Infantry School.

Military Affairs. Washington, D.C.: American Military Institute.

Military Review. Fort Leavenworth, Kan.: U.S. Army Command and General Staff College.

Index

AAF; *see* Army Air Forces
AAFSS; *see* Advanced aerial fire support systems
ACSFOR; *see* Force Development
ACSI; *see* Intelligence
ACTIV; *see* Army Concept Team in Viet-Nam
Adams, John, 4
Adjutant General, 53, 62, 64
Adjutant General's Corps, 65
ADP; *see* Automatic data-processing
Advanced aerial fire support systems (AAFSS), 179–80
Aeronautical Division (of Signal Corps), 142–43
AFSTRIKE; *see* Air Force Strike Command
AGF; *see* Army Ground Forces
Air Force, 19, 20, 39, 73, 117–18, 124, 127–28, 146–53; and conflict with Army, 144 ff.; *see also* Air Force, Department of
Air Force, Department of, 56, 120, 146; *see also* Air Force
Air Force Strike Command (AFSTRIKE), 127–28
Air National Guard, 158
Air power: in World War I, 143; in World War II, 146; post-World War II, 146–47
Airborne divisions, 36
Aircraft: C-5A, 150, 151; C-54, 151; C-130, 150; C-135, 150; C-141, 150; CH-37, 74; CH-54 Flying Crane, 180; Chinook, 175; Huey Cobra, 180; Iroquois, 175; Mohawk, 81; VSTOL, 180; VTOL, 152–53, 178–79, 180; XC-142,

180; *see also* Helicopters
Airlift, 87, 129
Airmobile divisions, 41–42, 172, 176
Alaskan Command (ALCOM), 129–30
Albanian Army, 96
ALCOM; *see* Alaskan Command
Allan, Ethan, 4
AMC; *see* Army Matériel Command
Antitank weapons, 183–84
ANZUS; *see* Australia–New Zealand–United States Treaty
ARADCOM; *see* Army Air Defense Command
ARLANT; *see* Atlantic Command
Armed Services Committee, 166–67
Armored divisions, 36, 37
Army Air Corps; *see* Army Air Forces
Army Air Defense Command (ARADCOM), 99, 132, 159, 163
Army Air Forces (AAF), 84, 144–46; *see also* Army aviation; Helicopters
Army Air Service; *see* Army Air Forces
Army aviation, 146, 148, 151–52, 178–80; *see also* Army Air Forces; Helicopters
Army Concept Team in Viet-Nam (ACTIV), 71
Army, Department of, 31, 161
Army Departmental Headquarters, 57
Army Forces Strike Command (ARSTRIKE), 100, 127–28
Army Ground Forces (AGF), 145–46

207

Army groups, 33
Army High Command, 145
Army-McCarthy hearings, 166
Army Matériel Command (AMC), 65, 67–68, 70, 85, 174
Army Reserve (USAR), 64, 66, 154–63, 166–67
Army School of the Americas, 101, 139–40
Army School Training Center, 66
Army, Secretary of the, 56, 64, 167
Army Security Agency (ASA), 65, 69
Army Service Forces (ASF), 84, 145–46
Army War College, 54, 55
Arnold, Benedict, 7–8
ARSTRIKE; see Army Forces Strike Command
Artillery, 7, 9 ff.
ASA; see Army Security Agency
ASF; see Army Service Forces
Atlantic Command (ARLANT), 99, 126, 130–31
Atomic weapons, 36, 75, 77, 93–94, 99, 146, 147
Audit Agency, Chief of, 64
Australia–New Zealand–United States Treaty (ANZUS), 100, 102
Automatic data-processing (ADP), 186
Aviation Section, 143

Balloon corps, 142
BARC (amphibious vehicle), 74
Battalion, 31, 40
Battle group, 37
Battle of Fallen Timbers, 11
Battle of Queenston Heights, 154–55
Beaumont, Dr. William, 26
Berlin Brigade, 135
Blitzkrieg, 73, 172
Board of War and Ordnance, 50
Body armor, 71
Brigade, 31, 177
Budget, Bureau of the, 168
Bulgarian Army, 96
Byrnes, James F., 106, 107

C-5A; see Aircraft
C-54; see Aircraft
C-130; see Aircraft
C-135; see Aircraft

C-140; see Aircraft
Cavalry, 10, 39
CDC; see Combat Developments Command
CENTO; see Central Treaty Organization
Central Intelligence Agency, 120
Central Treaty Organization (CENTO), 100–101
CH-37; see Aircraft
CH-54; see Aircraft
CH-74; see Aircraft
Chaparral; see Missiles
Chaplains, Chief of, 62
Chaplains' Corps, 65
Chemical Corps, 66
Chief of Staff, 56, 57 ff., 84, 85, 167
China, People's Republic of, 93–96
China, Republic of, 102–3
Chinook; see Aircraft
Civil War (American), 14, 142, 172
Civilian Conservation Corps, 19
Civilian control of the Army, 48–52
Clark, Lieutenant William, 21–22
Combat command, 38
Combat Developments Command (CDC), 65–67, 70
Combatant Commands, 125–40
Combined Chiefs of Staff, 119
Communications, 79–81, 185–86
Communications-Electronics, Chief of, 62, 68–69, 70
Company (troop unit), 30–31
Comptroller of the Army, 61, 64, 167–68
Computerization of equipment, 88, 89
CONAD; see Continental Air Defense Command
CONARC; see Continental Army Command
Congress: Armed Services committees, 166–67; establishes Army Air Forces, 144–45; establishes Army Air Service, 143–44; establishes Army Reserve, 160; Army-McCarthy hearings, 166; establishes Aviation Section, 143; passes Dick Act, 156–57; Legislative Liaison, Chief of, 167–68; and Marshall Plan, 107; establishes Medical Reserve Corps, 160; establishes National Guard, 155–56; National

Security Act of 1947, 117 ff.; relationship with Army, 164–70; after Revolutionary War, 9, 48 ff., 117; before Revolutionary War, 3 ff.; and War of 1812, 11
Continental Air Defense Command (CONAD), 126, 131–34
Continental Army, 3–5, 49, 112
Continental Army Command (CONARC), 65–66, 67, 69, 70, 127–28, 130
Corps, 32, 33
Corps of Engineers, 11, 23, 28, 65, 83, 165
Counterinsurgency, 104–6, 108–16, 123
Counterinsurgency and Special Activities, Special Assistant for, 123
Cuban missile crisis, 59, 95, 130
Czechoslovakian Army, 96

"Davy Crockett"; see M-28
DCSLOG; see Logistics, Deputy Chief of Staff for
DCSOPS; see Military Operations, Deputy Chief of Staff for
De Gaulle, Charles, 101–2
Defense, Department of, 30, 120, 168
Defense, Secretary of, 50, 56, 120 ff.
Dick Act, 156–57
Division, 31–32, 33; airborne, 36; airmobile, 41–42, 172, 176; armored, 36, 37; cavalry squadron, 39; infantry, 31 ff.; mechanized, 39; pentomic, 36–38; ROAD, 38–42, 176, 187; square, 34–35, 36; triangular, 35–36, 37
Downwash, 180–81
Duportail, Louis, 6

East German Army, 96
"Educational" contracting, 86–87
XVIII Airborne Corps, 128
Eighth Army, 136–37
Eisenhower, Dwight D., 175
Electronics Command, 68
Engineers, Chief of, 62, 168
Engineers, Corps of, 11, 23, 28, 65, 83, 165
Eskimo Scouts, 129
European Command (USEUCOM), 134, 135

European Theater (of World War II), 33
Explorer I, 24

Fallen Timbers, Battle of, 11
FASCOM; see Field Army Support Command
Field army, 32, 33
Field Army Support Command (FASCOM), 85–86
Finance, Chief of, 64
Finance Corps, 65
Firepower, 72, 74
1st Cavalry Division (Airmobile), 41, 42, 176, 187
1st Expeditionary Division, 34
Flying Crane (CH-54); see Aircraft
"Flying jeeps," 146
Force Development (ACSFOR), 61
Foreign Assistance Act; see Marshall Plan
Forrest, Lieutenant General Nathan B., 72
Freedmen's Bureau, 17

General in Chief, 52–53
General Staff, 55 ff., 83
Grant, Ulysses S., 53
Green Berets; see Special Forces
Green Mountain Boys, 4
Greene, Nathaniel, 8
Guerrilla warfare, 104–6, 108–16

Hamilton, Alexander, 7, 11
"Handie-Talkie," 89
Hawk; see Missiles
Helicopters, 41, 71, 74, 152, 178–79; "fighter" helicopters, 179; in Korean War, 73, 148; in Viet-Nam, 73, 172, 179; see also Aircraft
Honest John; see Missiles
Huey Cobra; see Aircraft
Hungarian Army, 96

Indians (campaigns against), 10–11, 18
Infantry, 3–8, 9, 31 ff.
Inspector General, 64
Insurgency, 105–6; see also Guerrilla warfare
Intelligence, Assistant Chief of Staff for (ACSI), 61, 62–63, 69

Intelligence and Security Branch, 66
Intelligence Command (USINTC), 65, 69
Inter-American Treaty of Reciprocal Assistance, 100, 101
Iroquois; see Aircraft

JCS; see Joint Chiefs of Staff
Jefferson, Thomas, 11
Johnson, Andrew, 160
Johnston, J. E., 14
Joint Army-Navy Board, 118, 119
Joint Chiefs of Staff (JCS), 56, 119 ff., 150
Judge Advocate General's Corps, 65–66

Kalb, Baron Johann de, 6, 7
KATUSA; see Korean Augmentation to the U.S. Army
Kennedy, John F., 114
Khrushchev, Nikita, 105
Knox, General Henry, 7, 11
Korea, Republic of, 102–3, 136; see also Korean War
Korean Augmentation to the U.S. Army, 136–37
Korean War, 15, 20, 51, 73, 105, 113, 147–48, 187
Kosciuszko, Thaddeus, 6

Lacrosse; see Missiles
Lafayette, Marquis de, 6, 156
Lance; see Missiles
LANTCOM; see Atlantic Command
Laos, 115, 173
Laser range finder, 81
Lebanon, 126, 128
Lee, "Light Horse Harry," 7
Lee, Robert E., 14
Legislative Liaison, Chief of, 167–68
Lewis, Captain Meriwether, 21–22
Lincoln, Abraham, 51
Little John; see Missiles
Logistics, 82–90
Logistics, Deputy Chief of Staff for (DCSLOG), 61, 62, 70, 85
Louisiana Purchase, 21–22

M-28 (recoilless rifle), 77
M-48 (tank), 74

M-60 (machine gun), 175
M-107/M-110 Group (self-propelled artillery), 182
M-548 (vehicle), 78
MAAG; see Military Assistance Advisory Group
MacArthur, General Douglas, 51
McClellan, General George B., 14
McDowell, General Irvin, 51
McKinley, William, 54
McNamara, Robert S., 94, 166
MACV; see Military Assistance Command, Viet-Nam
Mahan, Dennis Hart, 12, 172
Main Battle Tank (MBT), 177–78
Major commands, 64–70
Manhattan Project, 25
Marines, 20, 117, 121, 123, 168
Marion, Francis, 113
Marsh Screw (amphibious vehicle), 182
Marshall, General George C., 107
Marshall Plan, 107
MBT; see Main Battle Tank
Mechanized division, 39
Medical Reserve Corps of the Army, 160
Medical Service, 65
Merrill, Brigadier General Frank D., 113
"Merrill's Marauders," 113
Metascope, 80
Mexican War (1846), 13–14, 118
Military Academy, U.S. (West Point), 11–13, 103
Military Airlift Command, 69
Military Assistance Advisory Group (MAAG), 139
Military Assistance Command, Viet-Nam (MACV), 109–10, 138
Military assistance program: in Latin America, 108; Marshall Plan, 107; in Viet-Nam, 108–12
Military colleges and academies, 161
Military District of Washington, 65
Military History, Chief of, 62
Military Operations, Deputy Chief of Staff for, 61–62
Military Police Corps, 66
Military Sea Transportation Service, 69
Military Traffic Management and

Terminal Service (MTMTS), 65, 69
Militias, 3, 4, 12, 14, 154–55
Mil-P-52469 (pump), 89
Miniaturization of equipment, 87–89
Missile Command, 68
Missiles: Chaparral, 78; Hawk, 78, 132, 185; Honest John, 38, 40, 78, 134, 184; intercontinental ballistic missiles (ICBM), 185; Lacrosse, 184; Lance, 134, 184; Little John, 40, 78, 184; Nike-Hercules, 78, 129, 132–33, 159, 185; Nike-X, 132, 185; Pershing, 78, 134; Polaris, 94, 99, 125, 176; Redeye, 78; SAM-D, 78–79, 133, 184; Sergeant, 78, 134; Shillelagh, 178; Sidewinder, 78; 66-mm. rocket, 78; Spartan, 185; Sprint, 133, 185; Zeus, 133, 185
Mission of the U.S. Army, 16–29
Mitchell, Brigadier General William L., 144, 146
Mobility Command, 68
Mohawk; see Aircraft
Morgan, General Daniel, 7
MQM-58A (airborne surveillance system), 186
MTMTS; see Military Traffic Management and Terminal Service
Munitions Command, 68

National Aeronautics and Space Administration, 22
National Defense Act of 1916, 157, 158, 161
National Guard Bureau, 64, 158
National Guard of the United States (NGUS), 64, 66, 129, 155–58, 161–63, 166
National Security Act of 1947, 56, 117, 119 ff., 146
National Security Council, 120, 121
National Security Resources Board, 120
NATO; see North Atlantic Treaty Organization
Navy, U.S., 11, 18, 20, 69, 73, 117–18, 168
NGUS; see National Guard of the United States
Nike-Hercules; see Missiles

Nike-X; see Missiles
IX Corps, 137
NORAD; see North American Air Defense Command
North American Air Defense Command (NORAD), 99, 131–34
North Atlantic Treaty Organization (NATO), 96, 100, 101–2, 107, 123, 134
North Korean Army, 97
North Vietnamese Army, 97
Northern Warfare Training Center, 129
Nuclear weapons; see Atomic weapons

Observation balloons, 142
173d Airborne Brigade (Separate), 177
Ordnance Corps, 66
Organization of Army units, 30–42
Osler, Sir William, 26
Ostfriesland, 144

Pacific Command (PACOM), 126, 135–39
PACOM; see Pacific Command
Pearl Harbor, 83
Pentagon, 30, 57, 71, 123, 154, 167, 168, 169
Pentomic division, 36–38
Pershing; see Missiles
Personnel, Deputy Chief of Staff for, 61, 62, 162
Personnel Operations, Chief of, 62
Philip of Macedon, 112
Philippines, 102–3, 105
Pike, First Lieutenant Zebulon, 22
Polaris; see Missiles
Polish Army, 96
Polk, James K., 51
Popular and Regional Forces (Viet-Nam), 111
Project 80, 59, 64–65, 66, 67, 70
Provost Marshal General, 62
Pulaski, Count Casimir, 6, 7

Quartermaster Corps, 65
Queenston Heights, Battle of, 154–55

Radar, 80–81, 131
R&D; see Research and Development

Redeye; *see* Missiles
Reed, Major Walter, 26
Regiment, 31
Reorganization Objective Army Division (ROAD), 38–42, 176, 187
Research and Development (R&D), 61, 63, 67, 70, 173–74, 182, 190
Reserve Components, Office of, 61, 63–64, 158–59, 162; *see also* Army Reserve
Reserve forces; *see* Army Reserve
Reserve Forces Act of 1955, 160–61
Reserve Merger Plan, 166–67
Reserve Officers Training Corps (ROTC), 62, 161–62
Revolutionary War, 3 ff., 50, 58, 113
Rio Treaty; *see* Inter-American Treaty of Reciprocal Assistance
ROAD; *see* Reorganization Objective Army Division
Rochambeau, Count Jean Baptiste de, 6
Rockets; *see* Missiles
Roosevelt, Franklin D., 84
Root, Elihu, 54–55
ROTC; *see* Reserve Officers Training Corps
ROTC Vitalization Act of 1964, 161
Rumanian Army, 96
Russia; *see* Soviet Union

SAC; *see* Strategic Air Command
SAF; *see* Special Action Forces
SAM-D; *see* Missiles
Scammel, Alexander, 7
Schofield, General John M., 53–54
Scott, General Winfield, 14
SEATO; *see* Southeast Asia Treaty Organization
Sergeant; *see* Missiles
SETAF; *see* Southern European Task Force
Seventh Army, 134
7th Logistical Command, 137
Sharp, Daniel, 105
Sheridan, General Philip H., 53
Sherman, General William Tecumseh, 53, 172
Shillelagh; *see* Missiles
Sidewinder; *see* Missiles
Signal Corps, 66, 142–43
66-mm. rocket; *see* Missiles

South Korea; *see* Korea, Republic of
South Viet-Nam; *see* Viet-Nam
SOUTHCOM; *see* Southern Command
Southeast Asia Treaty Organization (SEATO), 100, 102
Southern Command (SOUTHCOM), 139–40
Southern European Task Force (SETAF), 135
Soviet Union, 93–96, 173, 178
Spanish-American War, 14, 54, 142
Special Action Forces (SAF), 114–15
Special Forces, 112–16, 139
Special Staff, 55, 58, 59 ff., 71
Special Warfare, John F. Kennedy Center for, 114
Specified Combatant Commands, 125–26
SPIW (rifle), 183
Sprint; *see* Missiles
Square division, 34–35, 36
Staff bureaus, 52–54
Staff system, 57–64, 83
Standardization of equipment, 87–89
STRATCOM; *see* Strategic Communications Command
Strategic Air Command (SAC), 125–26, 127
Strategic Communications Command (STRATCOM), 65, 68
Strategy, 91–106
Strike Command (USSTRICOM), 126–28, 150
Supply; *see* Logistics
Supply and Maintenance Command, 68
Support Services, Chief of, 62
Surgeon General, 62
"Swamp Foxes," 113

Table of Organization and Equipment (TOE), 31–37, 40
Tactics, 72–74
Task force, 33, 126
Taylor, General Zachary, 14, 51
Technical Intelligence Division, 174
Television, 63, 80
Test and Evaluation Command, 68
Thailand, 139, 173
Thayer, Major Sylvanus, 12

III Corps, 128
TOE; *see* Table of Organization and Equipment
TOW (antitank system), 183
Training, 65
Transportation Corps, 66
Triangular division, 35–36, 37
Truman, Harry S., 51, 106
25th Infantry Division, 138

U.N.; *see* United Nations
Unconventional warfare, 97, 103, 104–6, 108–16
Under Secretary of War, 83, 84
Unification of Armed Forces Act, 56, 165
Unified Combatant Commands, 49, 126–40
Union Army of the Potomac, 142
United Nations (U.N.), 106
U.S. Army Alaska (USARAL), 129–30
U.S. Army Europe (USAREUR), 102, 126, 134–35
U.S. Army Forces, Southern Command (USARSO), 139–40
U.S. Army, Japan, 137
U.S. Army Pacific (USARPAC), 136–39
U.S. Code, 16
U.S. Information Service, 109
U.S. Mission, Viet-Nam, 109
U.S. Operations Mission, Viet-Nam, 109, 111
USAINTC; *see* Intelligence Command
USAR; *see* Army Reserve
USARAL; *see* U.S. Army Alaska
USAREUR; *see* U.S. Army Europe
USARPAC; *see* U.S. Army Pacific
USARSO; *see* U.S. Army Forces, Southern Command
USEUCOM; *see* European Command
USSTRICOM; *see* Strike Command

Van Rensselaer, General Stephen, 154–55
Vehicles, 181–83
"Vertical artillery," 73
"Vertical envelopment," 73
Veterans' Reserve Corps, 160
Viet-Cong, 111, 113, 139
Viet-Nam, 15, 41, 42, 71, 73, 79, 92, 97, 109–16, 135, 138–39, 172–73, 177, 179, 187, 189, 190
Virginia, Army of, 51
Von Steuben, Baron Friedrich Wilhelm, 6, 7, 112
VSTOL; *see* Aircraft
VTOL; *see* Aircraft

War College, Army, 54, 55
War Department, 50, 84, 117
War of 1812, 11, 51
War, Secretary of, 50, 51, 52 ff.
Warsaw Pact, 96, 173
Washington, George, 4–5, 6 ff., 15, 49, 105
Wayne, General Anthony, 7, 10–11
Weaponry, 73–79
Weapons Commands, 68
West Point; *see* Military Academy, U.S.
Westmoreland, General W. C., 138
Whiskey Rebellion, 105
Whitney, Eli, 23
Women's Army Corps, 66
Wool, John E., 14
World War I, 34, 83, 143, 155
World War II, 20, 33, 35, 73, 113, 118–19, 155; Army aviation in, 146; Army Reserve in, 160; joint operations in, 119; logistics in, 83–85; National Guard in, 159; tactics in, 73

XC-142; *see* Aircraft
XM-561 (truck), 182

Zeus; *see* Missiles